When Tragedy Strikes

Laura's book, When Tragedy Strikes, *will squeeze tears from your eyes and put a smile on your face as she writes about her beautiful daughter, Becca, and the process she experienced from pain to purpose. Having lost my own daughter at Columbine in 1999, I understand the sorrow of an unimaginable loss. This is a book that should be read by everyone who has experienced the loss of a loved one, especially a child.*

Darrell Scott, founder of Rachel's Challenge, and author, father of Rachel, age seventeen

Seldom have I read a book written with such honesty, frankness and passion regarding the struggles one encounters when a loved one has died. Although written after the death of her daughter Laura's journey of moving through loss to again find hope has pearls of wisdom for recovering from any loss.

Dr. Gloria Horsley, president and founder of www.opentohope.com and mother of Scott, age seventeen

If you have suffered great tragedy and struggle to connect with God in your grief and disappointment, When Tragedy Strikes *was written for you. Laura Diehl knows the unfathomable pain of losing a child in tragic circumstances, and through the grief and pain finding her footing in the love of an affectionate Father. As she describes her own journey with honesty, compassion, and wisdom, she will help you process your own journey and find a glorious hope beyond your darkest days.*

Wayne Jacobsen, author of *He Loves Me, Learning to Live in the Father's Affection*, and co-writer of *The Shack*, Lifestream.org

As a mother of a beautiful baby boy, who lives in Heaven, I found When Tragedy Strikes *to be comforting and encouraging. As I read through the chapters, many aspects of the book sounded familiar to my own grief; the many questions and thoughts I have experienced. I have had many doubts and questions to why God would let my family go through such pain and loss, but reading through this book helped me realize that it's okay not to know all the answers, and to have hope that the future can be bright again, to be open to God's plan for me and my family, and that there is light at the end of the tunnel.* When Tragedy Strikes *also reminded me that I need to take care of myself physically and mentally to be able to carry myself through my journey.*

Leanne Steinberger, mother of Daniel, nine precious days

As a mom who lost her son two years ago, I thought I was never going to get through it. When Tragedy Strikes *is a very powerful book and I am so glad I read it. I was surprised at how often Laura put into words things I have experienced and thoughts I have had. It has helped me to realize that it's okay to still have good days and bad days. I call* When Tragedy Strikes *the healing book.*

Donna Ames, mother of Josh, age twenty-six

The most harrowing experience a mother endures is to bury a child and not lose her mind or abandon her faith. Walk with Laura and be encouraged as she shares the story of losing her precious Becca and discovering a resolve that comes only after trusting God in the deep, dark throes of grief.

Shelley Ramsey, author of *Grief: A Mama's Unwanted Journey*, mother of Joseph, age seventeen

From my perspective as a pastor and walking through every season of life with thousands of people, the death of a child has to be the most excruciating loss a person can go through. The pain seems unstoppable and all consuming. And then you add on top of that the stupid and flippant responses people make to you as a grieving parent, and it further entrenches you in a dark forest without a compass and without a light. In the book When Tragedy Strikes, *Laura is able to skillfully give voice to this grief in a loving and poignant way that only a person who has gone through the death of child can fully understand. But in addition, she is able to create a tangible blueprint for rebuilding your life that will give you a compass and a light to guide you through the darkness of your grief. If you are walking through the death of a child, or someone near you is walking through this,* When Tragedy Strikes *is a must read.*

Russ Walker, senior pastor of CrossPointe
Community Church

The way Laura has chosen to allow her words to dance out the beauty of joy and sorrow that grief inevitably is, just takes my breath away. She has allowed her heart to find the friend grief can become, if we embrace the barren sorrow of pain and allow ourselves to be emptied, so that we can once again be filled. She has reached out a hand in the book When Tragedy Strikes, *and allowed her readers to experience her grief like a child would experience their first trip to the sea, watching its waves roll back and crest the edge of the sand; witnessing the power of its capacity to drown us, but reveling in the sweet sensation of floating above the waves in our daddies arms. That is the picture Laura has painted for me. She has given me eyes to see beyond the drowning pain of losing a child and allowed me to witness the resurrection power of the human spirit within the arms of Jesus Christ. It is an honor to know her story and to have seen her craft it so deeply, so sweetly, so tragically gorgeous, as she chose to allow the years soaked in tears to become a garden of gratefulness. I raise my glass to you, mama. I am grateful for you.*

Hannah Linton, singer, writer, grief counselor,
and mother of three on earth and seven in heaven (five
miscarriages, one stillborn, and one ninety minutes old)

Wow! Talk about taking off the masks. It's absolutely amazing how revealing and authentic When Tragedy Strikes *is. Laura Diehl is very real and open about the depth of darkness she was in when her daughter died. I truly admire her willingness to expose the ugly internal turmoil which those of us who have not lost a child to death know nothing about. And yet we are not left in that place of darkness with her, but we rise up with hope and life in the arms of a faithful God. I have been honored to be a part of Laura's journey and believe many will be touched by God's goodness they will read about in these pages, receiving hope and life for whatever situation they find themselves in.*

Dr. John Veal, senior pastor of Enduring Faith Christian Center, Chicago, CEO of John Veal Ministries

Laura Diehl has a way of sharing her experience and healing after hers daughter's death that is so relatable. Your heart and soul can't help but be touched by her honesty and openness about her hurt and depression. I believe this book will help so many people. When Tragedy Strikes *touches all aspects of the grieving process and brings Scripture and life experience together. We are not going through this alone. Not only do we have our Father in heaven holding us up, but he has given people like Laura the gift and inspiration to share with us the hope and healing we need.*

Kathy Pelton, mother of Joshua, age 23

After years of struggling with the death of my son and daughter, When Tragedy Strikes *completely validated my emotional journey. Laura's willingness to expose her true thoughts and feelings made me feel justified, not ashamed of my own feelings. She focused my head and heart on the only true Healer who can provide all I need in the midst of my dark valley —Jesus Christ. I am hopeful for the day I will be reunited with my precious babies. Thank you Laura, for writing this book, and giving me and all grieving parents a voice in the midst of our pain.*

Laurie Bolka, mother of Nelson, 4 months and Jessica, 2 months

Laura worked faithfully for our ministry for over 10 years. During that time there were many health crises with her daughter Becca. We prayed with her and supported her. But as she clearly details in this book, unless you've had one of your children die you can't possibly understand the grief a parent goes through. Reading When Tragedy Strikes *has made me realize how much more there was to the story than we understood at the time, even though from a distance we walked through it with her. Laura and Dave are tremendous parents who have come out the other end of this tragedy amazingly victorious. I have the highest respect for them, and I highly recommend this book to anyone who is struggling with the death of a child as Laura did.*

Becky Fischer, founder/executive director
of Kids in Ministry International and The School of
Supernatural Children's Ministry

I am not a very big reader, but my wife asked me to read the chapter written by Dave. It was definitely something I could relate to from another father and believer's point of view. I found it encouraging and uplifting, and was thankful my wife shared it with me.

Michael Steinberger, father of Daniel,
nine days old

Author Laura Diehl presents in her writing an honest account of a long slow ordeal: because this life trial transcends pain and loss and becomes an inspiration. When Tragedy Strikes: Rebuilding Your Life With Hope and Healing After the Death of Your Child *offers a vision of a life well-led and of love in the thick of crisis and loss. Beyond inspiring.* When Tragedy Strikes *is an invaluable, compassionate, and spiritual harvest of redemptive insights that will both inspire and challenge the reader. I will recommend and share with many of my personal and professional friends.*

J.P. Olson, author of ***Voices Out of The Box***
and founder of Journey Into The Word Ministries

With brutal honesty, Laura walks her reader through the anguish and heartache of losing her adult child. However, more than that, she continues her journey to the other side of grief and recovery. Through it all her faith shines through.

Janice Pitchford, speaker and author of **Finishing Well-My Daughter's Journey Home** and mother of Dawn, age fourteen

If you are a parent who has experienced the death of a child, you know the searing devastation and pain of this unspeakable loss. In this book, Laura proposes that two deaths occurred that day: your child died, and so did you. The "you" that existed before that tragic day died with your child, and the "you" who is left behind must find a new way to live. In When Tragedy Strikes, *Laura offers hope and encouragement, and shows a path that leads out of the darkness, and into new life. You can live again. Laura can show you how.*

Ray Edwards, founder of Ray Edwards International

I read When Tragedy Strikes *all in one setting. I can't express how amazing this was to read. Laura's story touched my heart and validated my experience when I embarked on the same journey 28 years ago when my son Joel Brian passed away. I feel this is required reading for any mother that is grieving the loss of a child.*

Pastor Lynn Breeden, founder of www.mourningtodancing.com, Joel Brian forever 5 years old

Laura Diehl and her family have gone through one of life's most painful tragedies imaginable, the loss of her beloved daughter, Becca. Through this book, When Tragedy Strikes, *Laura shares her heart with such transparency and openness about her life before and after the tragedy. I was quickly drawn into the book as if I experienced this journey with her. I highly recommend this book to anyone who has experienced tragedy on any level. Laura will inspire you with her faith and trust in the Lord Jesus Christ, who has ministered to her throughout her journey.*

Andrea Hall, Home Health Care Nursing
Assistant and Ordained Minister

When Tragedy Strikes

REBUILDING YOUR LIFE WITH HOPE AND HEALING AFTER THE DEATH OF YOUR CHILD

Laura Diehl

NEW YORK

When Tragedy Strikes

Rebuilding Your Life with Hope and Healing after the Death of Your Child

The Morgan James Speakers Group can bring authors to your live event. For more information or to book an event visit The Morgan James Speakers Group at www.TheMorganJamesSpeakersGroup.com.

Shelfie

A free eBook edition is available with the purchase of this print book.

ISBN 9781630477783 paperback
ISBN 9781630477790 eBook
Library of Congress Control Number:
2015914691

CLEARLY PRINT YOUR NAME ABOVE IN UPPER CASE

Instructions to claim your free eBook edition:
1. Download the Shelfie app for Android or iOS
2. Write your name in UPPER CASE above
3. Use the Shelfie app to submit a photo
4. Download your eBook to any device

Cover Design by:
Chris Treccani
www.3dogdesign.net

Interior Design by:
Chris Treccani
www.3dogdesign.net

In an effort to support local communities and raise awareness and funds, Morgan James Publishing donates a percentage of all book sales for the life of each book to Habitat for Humanity Peninsula and Greater Williamsburg.

Get involved today, visit
www.MorganJamesBuilds.com

Habitat for Humanity®
Peninsula and
Greater Williamsburg
Building Partner

DEDICATION

〰〰〰〰〰〰〰〰〰〰

To my sons: Christopher, Jamison, and Austin. Even though you have had to work through the tremendous pain and grief of losing your oldest sister, you reached out to me in the depth of my pain and darkness, not allowing my grief to consume me. You have made sure our life as a family has stayed intact, and brought much needed healing to my soul. I am so thankful God hand-picked each one of you for my life. I love you and am proud and honored to be your mother.

To my daughter: Kimberly, I am so thankful God hand-picked you as well to be my daughter, allowing me to carry you and give you life. I am also thankful you have been able to go forward and grow in the callings and giftings in your life, in spite of the pain of losing your sister here on this earth. I love you and am proud and honored to be your mother.

To my hubby: Dave, there are no words to say how much I love you and how much you mean to me. Thank you for holding me while I cried after I typed the final words to this manuscript. Thank you for giving me the grace I needed in my place of deep darkness. Thank you for choosing me to be your wife. I am so very honored and blessed to have you as my life partner.

To Becca: I love you, Becca-Boo. I have no words, just tears. Until we meet again…

Rebecca Kelly (Diehl) Howard

April 13, 1984-October 12, 2011

CONTENTS

\|\|\|\|\|\|\|\|\|\|\|\|\|

PREFACE

I have been wanting and needing to write this book for quite some time. I allowed anything and everything to distract me from that goal, most likely because I knew deep down how painful it was going to be.

Just trying to come up with a subtitle, the tears started flowing. I tried to use the word *pain*, but we all know what we feel after the death of our child is way too intense for such a simple, generic word. Is there even a word that exists to describe how we feel after the death of our child? It doesn't matter how old, it doesn't matter how young, it is so deep...so intense... so very wrong!

I found myself trying to think of a word to describe what I feel, and the only thing that came to me is *death*—the pain of my own death. A part of us dies along with our child. And yet somehow we must find a way to live again, especially those of us who have other children. There are people who miss us; there are people who need us.

But how do I do that? I am not "me" anymore. It is impossible to be that person.

There are things in this book that no one knows have been inside of me, not even my wonderful, loving, compassionate husband, Dave. He will find out some of these things himself, when I hand it to him to read over, once I have it all down on paper. And there are some things that I'm still not ready to share and maybe never will.

As grieving parents, we all have different thoughts and reactions. For instance, there are those of us who had children with extended hospital stays because of health issues. Some of us will now gravitate to TV shows with a lot of emergency situations or hospital scenes, while others will have absolutely nothing to do with them.

Even within myself I can have a different reaction to the exact same thing, such as songs on the radio. One day I can crank up a song and sing with it at the top of my voice, and the next time I hear the same song I can't turn it off fast enough before I feel the stabbing pain and I'm fighting tears. I have found it interesting that when Dave and I are in the car together, every once in a while one of us will reach up and turn the station. Nothing has to be said; we just know it's a song the other one can't listen to at that moment.

Because the grief of losing a child affects us in such different ways, you might not agree with everything I've written here. We might have different opinions, we might have different theologies. But I believe the common ground of the death of our children is a bond that extends beyond the differences.

And I believe you will find hope and encouragement to be able to live again through your own death that came from losing your child.

If you find a few tears falling while reading this book, I completely understand, because many tears fell while writing it.

ACKNOWLEDGMENTS

‖‖

I am not going to crank out a long list of people. However, there are a few I want to recognize and honor who were instrumental in this book being in your hands (or on your electronic reading source).

First I want to thank Ray Edwards. He invested in me, believed in me, gave me clarity in laying the foundation of the ministry God has asked my husband and me to steward, gave me the tools I needed to write my very first book, *Triple Crown Transformation*. And it was through a divine connection at his Permission to Prosper event in San Diego where I met David Hancock, the founder of Morgan James Publishing. Thanks, Ray, for the anointing you carry to push people to serve God with excellence and for all that you do for others. Great grace to you!

I want to say thank you to David Hancock, who took the time to talk with me at the event, asked me to send him what I had written so far, and got the ball rolling on getting this published; also to the team at Morgan James Publishing. Each one of you was there every step of the way to help me with this very tender and precious project. I never could have done this without any of you.

Angie Kiesling, I am so thankful you were available to be my editor. I believe you were sent by God to help me make this book the best it could be. May God richly bless you!

My mom, Mary Davis, spent a lot of time doing more than one pre-edit of the manuscript. I enjoyed the extra connection it gave us, and I thank you so much for the time and work you so willingly and lovingly put into this book. Sorry about the extra tears…

And it should go without saying, but I will say it anyway. I give God all the glory and all the honor, because without Him, not only would this book not be written, but I would not have a life worth living.

INTRODUCTION:

|||||||||||||||||||||||||||||||||||||

Facing the Debris

Where or how do we even start?

As parents, with the death of our child we can feel stuck in a very deep dark place. And I have found within that there is a second problem. We are not sure if we want to come out of that place. We want to stop hurting so deeply, but we are afraid if the pain goes away, we will forget our child, and that just isn't acceptable.

I was in that place myself. I have four other children and grandchildren. I didn't want to miss out on their lives, but I didn't know how to come out of this black hole that kept sucking me back down. As grieving parents, we know we are missing out on life that is continuing on around us, but the fog and pain are so strong it's like we don't care. And yet we do care. So much confusion…so much pain…too much to think about through our fog. Sometimes all we can do is breathe into the next minute.

For a long time I was either shut up in a room somewhere isolating myself in pain, or just going through the motions of living. Part of me died when my daughter died, and I felt that numbness of death for quite a long time.

When my daughter Becca left this earth, I didn't know anyone who had lost a child. There was no one I could go to, to find out if I was going crazy. As I found myself on this unwanted horrible path, I was contacted by someone I didn't know. She had lost her baby as an early stillborn delivery. She was devastated and needed someone who could cry and grieve with her in a way the people around her could not. Somehow, she heard about me on Facebook and sent me a message. Reaching out to her was very healing for me, and it helped more than I realized at the time.

Shortly after that, a friend of mine lost her son in a car accident. And a few months after that, one of my very best friends lost her son-in-law in a bizarre accident in a grain silo. (I realize that is not the same as losing your own child, but it was still someone reaching out to me for help to get through her painful journey.)

God in His faithfulness and great love used these others reaching out to me as a way to tug on me. I started to realize I wanted to be there for others in a way that no one was there for me. *When Tragedy Strikes* is my way of sharing some of the things I have learned through those dark times. Sometimes I have fallen off that dark cliff and battled the ugly monster of depression, other times I have been able to avoid it. When I have once again fallen into the dark pit, I have learned to check certain things within myself. When I do this, I find I spend a little less time there and am able to get out a little quicker than the time before.

These are the things talked about in this book. Things like our thoughts and words, our usefulness, our fears, being able to forgive, entering into rest (which is more than just sleeping), having hope, and so on.

As I was writing about all these things, somehow it sort of morphed into each topic becoming part of a house. That structure was unintentional at the start of the book, but as the writing progressed, every issue became part of the process of rebuilding a house—or, more appropriately, a home, since that is where the intimacy of our lives is lived.

Each of us has our own story. The circumstances that brought us to this place of grieving the loss of our child are different. Because of that, what brings me comfort may be very painful for you. Something that hurts me to think about might make you feel some relief in the details of your situation. I pray that does not cause any kind of disconnect between us while you read this book. I can never fully relate to your exact loss, but I can definitely relate to what many professionals consider the ultimate loss and the hardest thing a person can ever go through in this life.

You might feel like you're not ready for this at all. I urge you to keep reading and follow along with me. Allow that glimmer of hope to light in your soul. Please don't feel overwhelmed and think you have to start tackling all of these "things." Just allow the Holy Spirit to give you hope in one or two areas that you can take to Him and cry out for His help. When you are ready, allow Him to show you the next area He wants to breathe life into. See these as tools in a toolbox. Don't dump them all out and try to use them all at once. They are to be taken out as needed.

Let's take this journey together, holding each other up, because we need each other. But before we go any further, allow me to share with you a little bit of the story that brought me to this place of being side by side with you as a grieving parent.

CHAPTER 1

‖‖‖‖‖‖‖‖‖

Our Becca

Three years ago today, I buried my daughter. The pain of watching my sons—who were twenty-seven, twenty-two, and sixteen years old—being pallbearers for their sister's casket is beyond what can be put into words. (I also have a husband and another daughter, who was twenty-five at the time.) Becca was one day short of being twenty-nine years and six months old, and was married, with a daughter who had just turned nine years old.

Becca was a vibrant, strong-willed child. She loved life to the fullest, and we are still finding out how many people she touched with her life. She had a great laugh, a deep love for God, and an anointing for leading and writing worship songs. She also knew how to accept people unconditionally. She was a fighter and a testimony to the faithfulness of God, even in the worst of circumstances.

It's sadly ironic that what was used to save her life at three years old turned out to be what caused her life to be cut short at twenty-nine. When Becca was three years old, she had bone cancer in her left leg. Her tiny little leg was amputated, and she had nine months of chemo. Several years down the road, the medical industry discovered that one of the drugs given to her had long-term effects of heart damage.

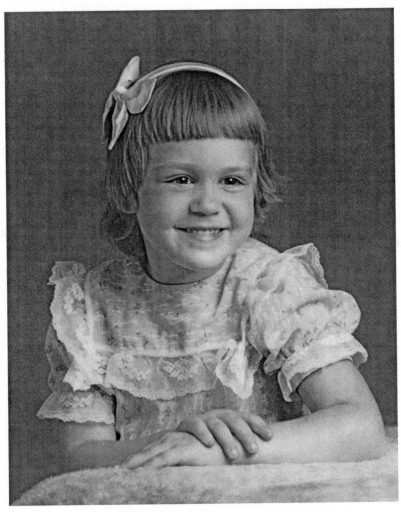

Becca at three years old pre-cancer

Becca on our first family vacation after the completion of her chemo

When we first had her checked, she had moderate heart damage, so they began watching it. As she reached the end of her teen years, the heart damage was heading from moderate into severe. Becca married young, at nineteen years of age, and became pregnant shortly after the wedding. The pregnancy put a strain on her heart, and she ended up living at the hospital while they monitored her. She was given only a 50 percent chance of surviving the labor and delivery.

I remember crying in my husband's arms as they took her back to have the baby early (since her heart couldn't handle the pregnancy much longer). I told him, "I know that I know that I know I trust God. I don't understand why I'm crying like this." In his wisdom, he knew exactly why I was crying. "Because we don't know which direction we're going to have to trust Him for." He was right.

Becca lived through it, and so did our little granddaughter.

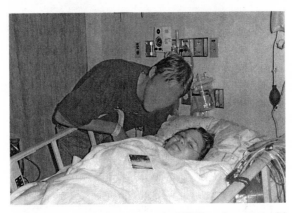

Their first family photo. Becca was in ICU and our granddaughter was taken to the neonatal unit, so all Becca had was this Polaroid picture of her daughter.

But from that point on, the heart issues escalated. She ended up at the Mayo Clinic for open-heart surgery for her valves. It helped for a couple of years but became a constant struggle for the doctor to have her on the right medications to keep her heart functioning properly.

In April 2010, my husband and I were in Tanzania doing children's ministry, and we got a call saying we needed to come home right away. Becca needed immediate heart surgery.

We flew home as soon as we could and, upon arriving at the hospital, found out she was refusing to have the surgery until we were there. They wanted to give the right side of her heart a pump called a VAD (Ventricular Assist Device) to keep it going. She needed to be put on the transplant list but was not healthy enough, so the VAD was considered a "bridge" until she could go on the list.

The next eighteen months were a roller coaster ride I cannot begin to describe in full detail, so I will just give the major events.

The Whirlwind Begins

A week after being dismissed from the hospital from getting the VAD, she had a stroke and had to be flown by helicopter back to her hospital (University of Wisconsin Hospital in Madison). From that point on, Becca was very limited in her mobility, used a motorized wheelchair, and needed help with almost everything, including getting on her portable bedside commode and washing up. (She grew up using a prosthesis, but as the heart problems escalated, the extra fluid from her heart issues caused her to gain too much weight for her leg to fit. So at this point she only had one leg and an almost useless left side of her body.)

Becca spent more than two-thirds of her last eighteen months in the hospital, including most holidays. She had at least a dozen ambulance rides and two more med-flight rides. The first one was because she caught the driveline of the VAD on something, slicing it, which caused the pump inside her to short out. That was horrible to watch, as the pump running her heart kept shorting out and jolting her. They opened her back up to remove the pump, because the driveline could not be repaired. By then the left side of her heart was having problems, but they could not give her a pump for both sides of her heart due to her individual circumstance. When she was healed from the surgery, she was sent home.

The third emergency medical flight occurred two months later. She was in the van with her husband and just fell over in her seat with Sudden Cardiac Death (SCD). He pulled over, called an ambulance, and they actually got her heart started! At our local hospital, Becca was put on ice (which is done after severe cardiac arrest in which the patient is unconscious, to help the body in several ways, including lessening damage to the brain) and flown back to Madison. There it was discovered she had also had a brain seizure. She was in the hospital for several weeks, and from that point on she wasn't the same.

About a month later, I took her up for an outpatient procedure and they ended up admitting her as a patient. At one point I had to call the nurse because Becca was getting delusional. Before I knew what was happening, they whisked her out of the room and took her to the Trauma Life Center. It is where the worst of the worst patients are taken, such as severe crash victims. Several hours later I finally found out she was in septic shock (blood poisoning), which only has a 20 percent survival rate. All of her organs had shut down and she was on total life-support systems. But, believe it or not, we saw another miracle and her organs began functioning again; she was eventually taken off all the life-support systems and released from the hospital.

Three days later, Becca ended up back in the hospital for a routine IV treatment for fluid overload. She was going to be dismissed from the hospital the next morning, but on the night of October 12, 2011, her heart finally gave out and she left us to go to her eternal home, to live forever with her Lord and Savior Jesus Christ.

Does it shock you to say I felt blindsided? God had given us miracle after miracle after miracle with her. I fully believed that she was either going to get healthy enough to receive a heart transplant, or God was going to miraculously give her a new heart without any surgery.

When I look back, I realize she knew she was going. I was away on another ministry trip at the time, and she kept asking me, on the phone from the hospital, when I was going to be home. I would ask her if she wanted me to come home early, and she would say no. But then she would ask me again when I was going to be home.

When I landed, I went directly to the hospital and spent two or three hours with her. I am an ordained pastor, and while I was there she wanted me to take my anointing oil and anoint her and pray over her. She specifically wanted me to give her a kiss on the forehead. And my last memory of Becca is the blessing of her lifting up her hand to return the "I love you" sign that I was giving to her while leaving the room. I knew something wasn't right, so after I made supper for the family, I decided to take the hour drive back to the hospital. I hadn't even gotten out of town when my son-in-law called to say that she had coded (her heart had stopped) and they were trying to get her back. So my return to the hospital ended up being to see her body…

Goodbye, My Daughter…for Now

To be honest, I don't know where to go from here in writing this chapter. I am sitting here in the silence, with tears streaming down my face, trying not to sob.

Broken—that's one word to describe how we feel as someone who has lost a child.

1. no longer whole; in two or more pieces
2. out of order; no longer in working condition
3. not kept; not honored or fulfilled

It sounds like a pretty good description of who we are now, doesn't it? We are wrecked, fragmented, shattered, cracked, smashed, and damaged—all synonyms of broken.

That is also the description of who Jesus came to save. Salvation isn't just the prayer that gets us into heaven. It is a continual process. Salvation comes from the Greek word *sozo* and means "to save, to deliver or protect, heal, preserve, be made whole." Most of us will look at that and want to scream, "Why didn't God do that for my child? I wish God would have saved my child instead of me! I can't bear this horrible pain!" I'm not going to give you any clichéd answers or start quoting scriptures to answer that question. But I will share with you my experience and, as we go along, share the things God has shown me when I asked those kinds of hard questions.

Now you know my story. So with that, let's get started. The first thing on my list is probably the hardest, but everything else seems to build on it. Let's check the very foundation of forgiveness.

CHAPTER 2

||||||||||||||

The Foundation of Forgiveness

When a child dies there can be so much unforgiveness it completely paralyzes a person. Many people—including strong Christians who have known the Lord for many years—find themselves angry at God, struggling or even refusing to forgive Him for allowing their child to die.

Sometimes we have to forgive ourselves, for a whole variety of reasons. We may also blame people who played a part in the final chapter of our child's life.

I think all of us have been surprised and hurt by family and close friends who seemed to abandon us when we needed them more than ever. I personally experienced a traumatic chain reaction that actually shocked me as much if not more than Becca's death itself, and call it the "domino effect". Or you may find yourself in a place similar to that of my youngest son, who discovered he had to forgive his sister for leaving him. (This is especially true when a child has committed suicide. I can't even begin to imagine how that leaves a parent feeling.)

Let's take a few minutes to look at these different types of unforgiveness together, starting with the need to forgive your child for leaving you.

Forgiving Your Child

Maybe this is a new thought for you. Maybe you have had this anger inside of you and didn't know where it was coming from; now this thought has opened your eyes to see what you couldn't before.

Not everyone has unforgiveness against their child. And many who do have a hard time admitting it. It sounds so awful and horrifying, but now you can be relieved to know you are not the only one who has felt this way. If this is you, I have a question to help you think about releasing your unforgiveness. Did he or she do this on purpose to hurt you? I hope the answer to that question is quite obvious, no matter what the cause of their passing was. Next question: Does anything good or even remotely constructive come from being angry at your child for leaving you? I think the answer to this question is obvious as well.

I understand how the pain of loss can be twisted into raw anger. I understand how wrong it is for our child to leave this earth ahead of us. But let's be angry at the situation, not our son or daughter who is no longer with us. If you want to get to the place where you can move beyond death and be able to live again, you will have to let go—to forgive your child for going on without you.

There is power in our words, much more than we seem to realize. Oftentimes, something we are thinking doesn't become a reality until we either hear it said or we speak the words ourselves. So I want you to forgive your child out loud for dying. Go ahead; it's okay, and you need to do this. It will probably be very painful, but in going through the pain you will be taking a step toward healing. Say it once; say it a hundred times if you have to. But say it.

_____, I forgive you for dying and leaving me here without you.

You may feel an immediate release, you may feel a deep stabbing in your heart, or you may feel nothing at all. But forgiveness is not based on a feeling, just like the love and care you gave to your child was not always based on a feeling. You love him because he is your son. You love her because she is your daughter. And in the same way, you forgive him or her.

Forgiving Others

I don't think there is a grieving parent who hasn't been surprised by some of the people they used to be very close to who are no longer a part of their lives. Have you had people either "unfollow" or "unfriend" you on Facebook after your child died? I have. These are people I thought would be there for me, but they don't call, they don't contact me, and when I make a feeble attempt to reach out to them, they either respond in a way that is very awkward or don't respond at all.

In our time of pain and fog, it can cause even more pain (as if that's possible) to have friends and family members pull away—like "rubbing salt" in our already gaping wound. Such actions cause many grieving parents to isolate ourselves even more than we do already.

There are so many reasons given for our friends and family reacting this way. The one I've heard most often is that being around us creates a fear in them that they could lose one of their own children, and so to ease their own pain/fear of that thought, they shut us out, often without realizing it. Another reason is that they don't know what to say or do, and to avoid the risk of hurting us they decide it's better to stay away and be silent.

Does it really matter why they no longer want to be a part of our lives? What if their reason doesn't make sense to us? Are we going to argue that excuse out of them? Would knowing their reason truly make us feel better? Do you really have the energy and perseverance to try to help them understand how much you need them right now? I sure don't.

The best thing we can do is to forgive them and let them go. In doing that, we release ourselves to begin to heal from this wound our friends and family did not intentionally give us. Once again, I encourage you to speak your forgiveness out loud. Let the forgiveness and the healing begin with your words, allowing the feelings to follow either right away or gradually, however it happens.

I mentioned the domino effects that were more shocking to me than Becca's death. One came when my other daughter totally rejected me, her dad, and her brothers. Some people in her life whom she loves and trusts were very influential in this.

At a time when our family was very fragile and vulnerable from Becca's death, my new pastor and his wife decided something was deeply wrong with me beyond the grief of losing my oldest child. The more I submitted myself to them and what they thought I needed for help, the further I went into depression. The grief became even heavier and the darkness blacker. The oppression was suffocating. I can't begin to describe the place I found myself in. I would spend hours and hours closed up in my tiny prayer room under the basement stairs, crying, resting, praying, crying, reading my Bible, journaling, crying, worshiping, even sleeping on the floor, and more crying.

One time when Dave and I went together to see the pastor and his wife for help, they told Dave it was his fault the family was such a mess, causing lots of confusion and tears. We found out later from our daughter that this conversation was secretly recorded and played for her to hear, to prove how unstable we were as her parents.

Around that same time, I also found out my daughter believed I wished it was her who died instead of her sister Becca! (I have since learned this is a common response of siblings as they watch the depth of their parents' grief.) I was totally stunned by that and could not convince her otherwise, especially alongside the confusion being brought into our family by this pastor and his wife, who by then had become my daughter's best friend.

As things escalated, our daughter hardly ever came home, not even to eat or sleep. This caused me to try even harder to "get her back." Since it was obvious to everyone I was getting worse instead of better, my daughter moved out of our home and in with the pastor and his family. The pastor's wife told me via a text that I was not welcome at church anymore—until I was ready to make things right and take responsibility for the division I was causing (based on some very serious false accusations).

My three sons and daughter-in-law refused to stay away from me as they were being told to do. Because they and my husband strongly disagreed with the pastors, and instead defended me, our daughter eventually broke off all communication with us.

The next few months were by far the most painful time of life I have ever been through. I felt like I had lost both of my daughters. This went on for several months, including not hearing from her over holidays and family birthdays. Here the rest of us were, now treasuring each other more deeply than we ever had before and desperately wanting her to be part of it, but instead we were cut out of her life.

Where are we now with this? At the writing of this book, we are in the healing process. I know it is God's will and desire to bring complete healing and full restoration. Sometimes it seems like three steps forward and two steps back, but I know God has the final say. Even if complete healing and restoration never occur here on this earth, they *will* happen before His throne in heaven someday.

I readily admit this situation is a constant battle of forgiveness in my heart. I am reminded of a controversial novel called *The Shack* by William P. Young that I have read several times. It tells the story of a man who has to deal with the murder of his young daughter. Through a series of events he is led to her body in a cave in the woods. God has already dealt with him in his unforgiveness of the man who took his daughter's life. As he is carrying her body, he occasionally mutters, "I forgive you...I forgive you..."

As I look back on what happened, part of what I see is a couple who may have meant well but did not even remotely understand, nor were they equipped to deal with, the legitimate depth of grief when a parent loses their child from this earth, or siblings lose a sister. The death of a sibling is like losing your compass in life; you have lost a huge piece of your past and at the same time lost a huge piece of your vision for the future. It leaves the surviving siblings very disoriented and lost.

The death of a child is the hardest slam a person can have in this life. It actually causes physical trauma to the heart and other organs of the body, along with changes in the brain. It affects us physically, emotionally, and spiritually (which I will explain in detail later, something God showed me about what happens to us spiritually when a child dies).

All this leads me to say, being a spiritual person doesn't automatically erase the painful effects of our child leaving this earth ahead of us. Every fiber of our being knows how wrong that is! Knowing that Becca is in heaven and I will see her again someday in glory does not bring a God-sized eraser and take away all the pain.

Psalm 23 says the Lord will be with us when we "go through the valley of the shadow of death." Grief is something we have to travel through before we can rise above it. I have often thought the pain of losing my child has no shadow. It is just a valley of death. I don't know of a single parent who has lost their child who has not taken at least three years to work their way out of this valley. (Although it feels more like a pit of death we are thrown into, not a valley we are walking through, with hungry lions of depression and darkness we fight against to be able to climb out.)

I believe forgiveness is one of the first steps to getting out of this pit, and it is not based on our feelings. It is a choice we make. When it comes to the death of our child, including the circumstances around it and the domino effects it may cause, we can discover we don't have what it takes within ourselves to forgive. But God already knows that, and He has made a way for us to be able to forgive in His strength—a strength far beyond our own.

Forgiving the "Guilty"

What about forgiving someone who had a direct impact on the death of your child, maybe even causing it? Or perhaps it was indirect, by not being there to stop something? I would say there is a pretty good chance you're spending a lot of time thinking about what that person did (or didn't do). And that is very understandable. But you won't be able to get through the grief if you don't first back up and allow the bitterness taking root in your heart to be removed.

You have one of two choices to make. You can keep dwelling on it, rehearsing all the reasons why you should remain bitter and why that person does not deserve to be forgiven, or you can choose to release that person in your thoughts and forgive them. I know these are just words—so easy to say, but so very hard to do!

It won't be a onetime thing but a process; sometimes a very slow and painful process. You will find yourself having to choose forgiveness over and over again. I know of one woman who took ten years of choosing to forgive the person who shot her son before the reality of forgiveness became a part of her life. Is it extremely difficult? Yes, for sure. Is it impossible? Only if you say so. It truly is your choice to hang onto unforgiveness and be destroyed by bitterness, or to start the process of forgiveness and eventually find freedom.

Most of us already know this, but it needs to be said here as a reminder. Forgiveness is not for the other person. It is for you. As long as you hold onto unforgiveness, you are chained to that person through your anger and bitterness. When you make the choice to forgive someone, you are not saying that you are okay with what they did and how they wronged you. Forgiveness does not depend on whether or not a person deserves that forgiveness. It isn't even based on if they are sorry for what they have done.

Choosing to forgive is refusing to no longer be dragged through the emotional mud by remaining attached to that person for the part they played in your child's death. Why would you want to stay connected to someone who has hurt you so deeply? Unforgiveness is not hurting them; it is hurting you like a cancer eating you up and killing your soul. Forgiving that person is not offering them a way out; you are giving yourself a gift. A gift you deserve to have and unwrap!

True love is not given based on an emotion, but a choice to remain committed unconditionally. Forgiveness is the same way. It is not based on emotions. It is a conscious decision we make that goes beyond our feelings. There is no question that the death of our child causes anger and pain, which is usually directed toward blaming at least one person we need to forgive.

Are you wondering who I find myself needing to forgive multiple times in direct relation to Becca's death? It is a doctor who came to see her a couple of weeks before she died. One reason she couldn't get on the transplant list was because she was overweight. Not being mobile made it extremely difficult to take off the sixty or so pounds they said she had to lose. I was with her when a doctor was sent to discuss some options to help her with this. One thing he told her was that if she *really* wanted to lose the weight, she could. He actually said, "Obviously I would not do it, but I could lock you up in a room and feed you nothing but bread and water, you *would* lose the weight."

At that point she pretty much quit eating. We couldn't even get her to drink protein shakes. Since the heart is a muscle, and hers was already so weakened and enlarged, it did not take very long for her heart to give out from lack of any nourishment, especially the lack of protein needed for her heart muscle to function properly. Yeah, I can't spend time thinking about that or I find myself getting angry all over again. "I forgive you…I forgive you…"

Don't play the blame game. It puts you on the devil's playing field, and the person who is guaranteed to lose is you, and everyone who loves you and still wants you and needs you in their lives.

Here we are again, at a place where you might have to speak forgiveness over someone who is responsible for the death of your child, causing such intense pain and grief. It may be someone who did it purposefully, or it could be the result of negligence. It could even be someone who is just a scapegoat—a person you can blame and direct your anger at—when it wasn't really their fault, including yourself.

Put that name in the blank and say this out loud whether you mean it in your heart or not. Remember, it is not about feelings. It is about setting yourself free from the chains that keep you attached to this person, which is preventing your healing.

> _____, **I forgive you for the part you played in the death of my precious child, _____. I don't forgive you because what you did (or didn't do) was okay. I choose to forgive you for my own sake, my own freedom and healing. I refuse to remain connected to you, allowing you to drag me around in this darkness and pain. I release your hold on me as I choose forgiveness.**

That probably won't be the end of it. You may need to come back to this statement of forgiveness multiple times a day at first. But as you determine in your heart to take these steps, God will be faithful to meet you. You will find yourself having to forgive this person less often, until one day you suddenly realize you truly have forgiven them and are free of the painful grip they once had on you. What a wonderful day that will be!

Forgiving God

Some parents think God took their child as a way of punishing them for something wrong they did in their past. If God punished us by killing our kids, we would see kids falling over dead just walking down the street. That is not who God is, that is not what God does. If you struggle with this belief, please drop those chains immediately! God did *not* use the death of your child as payback for something bad you did—some sin you committed. Would you do something as horrible as that to your own children? What kind of loving parent would do something so devastating? Even though we may not understand it, even though we may be angry about it, even though we know God is big enough that He could have stopped what happened, He did not use your child as a punishment against you. You did not cause your child's death by not living up to God's "rules."

Forgiveness is at the very core of God's being. He is the ultimate example of forgiving. His Son was tortured and murdered, and yet He forgave those who did it. Sometimes I admit I have had thoughts along the lines of "but there was a purpose in it. He knew what was behind the cross and the greater good that was going to come from it. I don't have that."

But then I stop and think about what I *do* know. I know that not only did God forgive those who murdered His Son, He forgave me. Because it is all my sin, all my despair and hopelessness, all my shame, my anger, and my dark thoughts that nailed Jesus to the execution stake He died on. He did that so I could be forgiven and spend my eternity in heaven with Him. But it wasn't just for something in the future. He did it so I could live my life on this earth in a forgiven state, so I can live my life from a place of freedom. So I don't have to remain in my sin, despair, hopelessness, shame, anger, and dark thoughts. He died so I could have LIFE, not just in heaven someday, but a fulfilled life while I am here on earth, no matter what trials come my way, including the most difficult one of all—the death of my child.

I can't trust someone if I believe they caused something negative and painful in my life. Neither can you. If you are blaming God for what happened to your son or daughter, you are going to have an extremely difficult time getting through this tragedy. Unforgiveness is toxic to every part of our being: our body, our soul (mind, will, and emotions), and our spirit.

Make the same choice to forgive God that I have asked you to make to forgive your child and others. Say it out loud. I'm not going to give you the words; let it come from your heart. If you are angry at Him, tell Him you are angry. He already knows it and He can take it! Let yourself feel the emotions. Take them to God. And tell Him even though you don't feel like it, even though you're angry and you don't understand, you choose to forgive Him for not saving your child from death.

Go ahead...I'll wait for as long as it takes (and so will He).

The foundation of forgiveness needs to be laid for you to start rebuilding your life. If you don't take care of it first, you are at high risk. It's like building a house on a sinkhole. You can find yourself with major repairs from an unexpected collapse a few years down the road, when you thought things were finally getting better.

I hope and pray you have taken this chapter to heart, laying the foundation of forgiveness, not based on how you feel, but on a choice you have made and spoken out loud.

Later in the book, I will share a second domino effect that shocked us. It left our family devastated and rocked our world for quite a while. But for now, let's go visit the garage. Why the garage? I'm glad you asked.

Have you ever pulled into your garage and for whatever reason remained in your car, not ready to go into the house? Well, I'm not quite ready to take you into the house yet, so let's go sit in the garage for a little while.

CHAPTER 3

||||||||||||||

The Garage of Tears

Some of the worst times are when I think I see Becca somewhere and get smacked once again with the crashing realization that it can't possibly be her. For me, the motorized scooter carts in a store still trigger the thought of my daughter. Even just hearing someone the next aisle over in one of those carts can give me a shocking reminder of my loss. I have had to fight tears so many times when I'm out shopping because of triggers like this. Sometimes I "win" and can escape without crying, and sometimes I don't as the tears spill down my cheeks. I wonder, why don't I ever see anyone else in the store who looks like they're crying? Or am I the only one who struggles with this?

There are so many bittersweet events now. Almost one year to the day of Becca's death, we had the blessing of a new little granddaughter coming into this world. She was given the name of Becca as a second middle name. And since then we've had another beautiful granddaughter born. They will never know their Aunt Becca. Like I said, bittersweet.

One of my sons got married six weeks before Becca passed away, and she was actually not in the hospital and able to attend the wedding. This is the only sibling who will have that blessing. The other three will be missing their sister, including the one who planned to have her as matron of honor someday.

She dreads the pain of that so much she is talking about just having a small gathering for a wedding and her sister's picture placed where she would have stood. Weddings are supposed to be a day full of joy and celebration. Like I said, bittersweet.

I feel the heaviness of grief trying to come in while writing this. So I will pause and think of my beautiful Becca in heaven, dancing with two legs, with Jesus. She is in the greatest celebration of all. I will remind myself that this earth is not my permanent home. "For the things which are seen are temporary, but the things which are not seen are eternal" (2 Corinthians 4:18). At some point, life on this earth won't matter, and we will all be united for eternity. What a glorious day that will be!

But until then, this is where we are, and we have to learn how to deal with life on this earth. The death of a child changes our lives, and it changes *us* more than anyone can even imagine. Only those of us who have experienced it can know what that means. And it is not that we are trying to elevate ourselves above someone who is grieving a different loss, such as a spouse or a parent. We would *gladly* not be a part of this elite club if there was any way possible to get out of it.

Those who have lost both a spouse and a child will say the death of their child far outweighs the death of their spouse. The length of the mourning process stretches out further. The loss of our child shatters the hope we had for their future. We have lost a physical extension of who we are. These are just some of the things that make this loss deeper when compared to other losses.

Is There Such a Thing as Grief Recovery?

In my searching for how to deal with my grief, I came across an article called "Grief Recovery." As I started reading it, I discovered it was for any kind of loss including jobs, moving, pet loss, death, divorce or any kind of breakup, starting school... Whoa! I don't think so! It talked about how recovery is when we can have memories without the pain. I had a hard time reading it without getting angry. It is just impossible to compare grieving the death of a child to all these other things. I'm not saying those things are not painful and that there is not a level of grief involved, but this article was basically saying after you grieve the right way, you can move on with life and put the past behind you.

I might be able to move forward, but it isn't by putting the death of Becca behind me! She will *always* be in front of me. Our children are our legacy. They are supposed to keep going when we leave this earth. Even if she isn't with me anymore, I can't leave her in my past and go on without her.

Even if we wanted to do so, the things that trigger us and remind us of our loss can come unexpectedly out of nowhere and bring back the memory, accompanied by unwanted pain once again.

I am a parent who took a lot of trips to the gravesite for probably a year or more. One day while I was there, the med-flight helicopter flew over me. I totally lost it and found myself sobbing uncontrollably. Later, I wrote on Facebook about what had happened, and a friend told me it was a sign of PTSD (Post Traumatic Stress Disorder). I guess it made sense.

For many, many months after Becca passed, whenever I heard an ambulance I would freeze in panic and my mind would immediately question, "Where is Becca?" And of course, there was always the realization of where she was, and the siren I was hearing was definitely not for her. Some days I am okay with that, other days…

The first year of special dates is always difficult for anyone who has lost a loved one, but for a parent who has a child missing it can be almost unbearable. For us, Thanksgiving came first and brought with it the memory of how the year before, Becca had insisted on hosting the family, even though she was wheelchair bound. Then came Christmas, Becca's favorite holiday, and then the pain of the first time she was not there to celebrate her birthday, and so on. Eventually it came around to the one-year anniversary of her death.

Everyone grieves differently, and I wanted to be sensitive to that. Some of the family wanted to get together and celebrate her life, and others didn't want anything to do with that. I was torn, and to be honest I don't even remember what ended up happening that first year for her birthday or the anniversary of her death.

The part I do remember, though, is now a precious tradition I share with Becca's daughter. That first year, my granddaughter asked what we were doing for her mom's birthday. Knowing how some of the family did not want to do anything, I suggested I come to her school for lunch on that day and bring birthday cupcakes for the two of us. She was thrilled, and we have been able to continue this. My granddaughter has been happy to have someone who wants to think about how much we love and miss her mom, remembering this special woman in both of our lives, and I have been happy to share that with her.

What I wasn't expecting was to have the second year be harder than the first! I see two reasons for this. First, I braced myself for those one-year markers. I knew they were going to be hard, so I tried to prepare myself for them mentally and emotionally. The second year it was more like I was caught off guard. *I've been through this before; it should be better this year,* I thought, so all of a sudden those dates were here and they just hit me like a brick wall.

Second, I was still in such a fog of unbelief the first year. So as the fog started to lift that second year, the loss was hitting me with full force. By the third year, it was more like a painful acceptance, trying to figure out how to live this new life without my daughter.

I feel like I need to say this to the parents who are still in deep grief. Do NOT look at any dates to see where I or others were emotionally in our grieving process and use it as some sort of a timeline to force on yourself. We are all on our own individual timeline and need to go through the process at our own speed. Yes, there are some "patterns" (for lack of a better word) that some of us seem to fall into, but don't expect yourself to fit into that. Give yourself grace to walk your own necessary path. As long as you are putting one foot in front of the other, you will get there.

In April of 1999, Dave and I took our two oldest children, Becca and Topher, to a Focus on the Family event called Life on the Edge. We were given what was called a "B-There Covenant" for us to sign, which the four of us did. Later in 2004, our other three children also signed it. This is now one of the most precious things I own. Let me tell you what it says.

B-There Covenant

We believe that when our life's journey comes to an end, the gates of Heaven will open wide and our Savior, the Lord Jesus Christ, will *B-There* to welcome us. The covenant we are signing today is a promise made to one another in the presence of God that we will

B-There in heaven for a glorious family reunion without end. From this point on, we are committed to love, accept, honor, forgive, pray for and encourage one another. We agree to treat each other with respect and kindness, and we pledge to resolve conflicts in a biblical way. We also promise to run the race, to persevere, and to fix our eyes upon Jesus, the author and perfecter of our faith.

Parent's B-There Promise

As your parent, I will most likely *B-There* before you. If I see Heaven before you, I will wait for you just inside the Eastern Gate. If you see Heaven before me, I will know you are waiting for me there. This is an appointment I will not miss!

Teen's B-There Promise

I promise to *B-There*. If I see Heaven before you, I will wait for you. If you see Heaven before me, I will know that you are waiting for me. This is an appointment I will not miss!

I never thought that part about one of my children "being there" before me would actually come to pass and was so very clueless as to how easy that sounded, compared to how hard it is to actually live it out. But I am so very thankful for this piece of paper, which is now framed and hanging on my "Becca" wall in our hallway, along with things like the photo of the butterfly hung on her hospital door the night she died.

Part of Becca's wall in our hallway

It has taken me an entire lifetime to learn that tears are a gift from God. Yes, I know some people can't seem to cry. But that is not the case for me. Tears have flowed freely and easily for me all my life. If I don't allow myself to cry, it means I have allowed my heart to get hard. I have done that before and will never do it again!

Jesus knew that when His dear friend Lazarus died, it was only temporary. And yet we know Jesus wept. If you want to cry, go ahead and cry as hard as you need to. Park your car in the garage and have a good cry. Let your tears be the gift God gave them to be, allowing them to wash away some of the pain.

You can go back to the garage anytime, and as often as you need to. You have full permission.

One of our family pictures taken over the years

CHAPTER 4

‖‖‖‖‖‖‖‖‖‖

The Family Room of a Support System

When a new baby is born there is so much excitement. There are announcements and pictures. We can celebrate for weeks as gifts and cards and visits continue. But when someone dies, as soon as the funeral happens, everyone goes back to life as normal.

Except for those whose lives are directly affected. And for those of us who have lost a child, life will never go back to normal. Unfortunately, on this earth death is a part of life. But for some reason our society won't allow us time to process the death of someone close to us. We can even lose friends over it. This can add to our pain and make it even harder to work through the grief of losing our child. As if that wasn't hard enough!

Circling the Wagons

Over the years, our family has gone through so many unusual and extremely painful situations, and whenever that happened we pulled together tightly as a family. (I realize not everyone has this blessing, but we made a strong effort not to allow our family to be splintered by difficult events.) In the pioneer days, when traveling out West, the pioneers used to "circle the wagons" when danger came, making it harder for someone or something to attack. That's a good illustration of what we would do as a family. Whenever a crisis hit, our immediate family (Dave, myself, and our five kids) would pull in tightly together. Then there were those who would circle around us, helping us close in for protection, such as our parents and our spiritual leaders. Then our closest friends would make a circle around them, and then came everyone else.

It was the "everyone else" we were often being protected from. Some were well-meaning friends who wanted to know what was happening and how everyone was doing. Some were people who seem to have a need to be in the middle of drama. We just did not have the energy or desire to communicate to so many people, so information would travel from our inside ring to the outer edges, which thankfully protected us from the drama people.

It's a given that those around us won't understand the pain of losing a child. But how sad it is to discover there are those who won't at least try to understand the depth of pain experienced when a child dies. Many people will abandon us in our grief because they think we're not "moving on" fast enough, or they feel we're "living too long in the past." Those kinds of toxic comments only add to our pain. Life doesn't just "go on as usual" after the death of a child. Our entire world is turned both upside down and inside out, and we will never be the same.

Like all grieving parents, I was emotionally unstable after Becca's death. Some of the very people who were in my life at the time—people who should have been part of my support system—did the most damage. Because we are still directly facing some of the effects of this, I will not go into all the details. But since it is part of this journey that sucked me into that deep dark place even further than I was already, I am sharing pieces of it.

Shortly after Becca's death, my pastor pulled me off the worship team and no longer allowed me to teach children's church. I was told I needed to be in a place of "rest" (that is why I had all those hours of alone time in my prayer room).

It was also decided that I had been under a demonic influence for many years, which was viewed as a big part of my problem. This belief caused me to have even more pain and confusion.

Being put in a place of so-called rest by my spiritual leader, forced into painful isolation during my time of deep grief, and then being under the belief of something so dark and serious by that same spiritual leader was *very* damaging.

Raw Emotions on Paper

Journaling has been an important part of my healing. I can say whatever I need to say, no matter how painful or ugly. I will be sharing some of my journal entries throughout this book. Let me start with this one, revealing the raw pain I was in during this time.

> 12/18/11: ...I just realized I can finally put into words how I've been feeling. I thought I was coming to a place I could soar; it was being spoken over me in multiple ways—but in the midst of that, I feel like I was chained and shackled by the very place and people I thought were going to help me soar. I don't understand it, and it is

painful.… I AM SO SICK OF CRYING! I AM
SICK AND TIRED OF FEELING LIKE I'M
NOTHING BUT A WEAK BABY!

I then went into detail about what was happening and
how my pastor was dealing with me during this time of grief.
Here is how that journal entry finally ended.

> …So kill me, God! Do it now, please! I
> lay myself on the altar. As I stretch out my hands
> to be nailed with Yours, I hear Your heart beat.
> And with each beat it says *I love you, I love you, I love
> you*…and with this, I can melt into Your peace as
> I melt into this heartbeat of love.

As I journal, I listen in my spirit for what I feel God is
speaking to me, and I write that down as well. Sometimes it will
become a conversation between God and me, which you will see
throughout the rest of this book. Here is what I heard God speak
to me in response to my dramatic thoughts above.

> *My beautiful child, lay back into My Son's
> death—your bridegroom and the lover of your soul. Lay
> back and rest. JUST BE! There is no striving—there is
> no trying to be anymore—there is no struggle in who you
> are. JUST BE in oneness with the Son. It is truly a place
> of rest as you become one with THE ONE who has done
> everything for you!*

I am very thankful my faith was not in a person, but
in God Himself. All but one of our family members who were

under that pastor were either pushed out or left, very wounded and having no desire to be part of any body of believers or under any spiritual leadership. A full healing is still in process with most of my family, but after about a year God restored me to have a desire to find fellowship again, and I am now in a place that is called to bring healing to wounded Christians, with a wonderful pastor and spiritual leadership team. God has also strongly reaffirmed my call to ministry, although it looks quite a bit different than it used to.

The strongest support most parents receive through the darkest times of grief is usually from other bereaved parents. That doesn't necessarily mean joining a formal support group, but finding some way to connect, even if it is just reading some books written by other parents who are on this path ahead of us. In today's world it is easy to connect through social media, which can also be helpful. In those places, we can just sit in silence and read what other parents are saying, or we can join in on any part of the conversation if the urge to say something is strong enough.

We find the love and camaraderie of each other much more healing than a counselor or psychologist. We don't need to be analyzed; we know what's wrong. We need comfort and hope from someone who has been where we are.

Some things I have read I can relate to, other things I cannot. I remember at one point reading about parents who didn't want to be around music anymore. Anything that brought a measure of joy or happiness would be denied. That was one I definitely could not relate to. For me personally, one of the best ways to receive comfort was just to sit and ask God to come be with me. I would put on worship music to surround myself with a soothing atmosphere of His presence and nearness. I would often cry through it, but it still definitely brought healing. I can't imagine a world with no music, but then again, that is a very good description of how we feel when we lose our child.

One of the things I read about that I could relate to is the horrible thought of my daughter buried underneath the ground. It's so crazy! I'm tearing up and trying to catch my breath just thinking about it even now. I *know* it's not really her; I *know* it is just her body. But as a mom, the feeling of your child being in such a cold dark place all alone... It's hard not to have that "mom protective instinct" to want to get your child out of there!

I encourage you to find someone who can understand your crushing pain, a pain so deep you feel like you can't even breathe at times. There is something deep inside us that needs to connect with others who have experienced what cannot be put into words. I remember reading about the specific need for connection to other parents in a book, and writing in the margin next to it "I NEED this!"

It is a rare but extreme blessing when you find someone who is not a bereaved parent who will allow you to lean into the grief. What do I mean by that? Someone who will allow you to let your grief take you where it takes you. They don't make you try to run from it, deny it, tell you that you need to be strong or that you should be past this by now. They don't quote scriptures and clichés. The intense pain from the death of your child is something you can't go around (no matter how much some people think you should). You must go *through* it to get to the other side. And you will need to have some people in your life who will allow that to happen. You might be blessed with a good friend who will stick by you and walk through this with you. Most of us have had to find another parent who is ahead of us on the same path in life who will walk through it with us.

Seeking Answers from the Spirit World: A Warning

Many parents turn to psychics at this time. This is extremely scary to me. Let me clarify my thoughts about this with a strong warning: there is definitely a spirit world, both good and evil. There is God and there is Satan. There are only two sources of the supernatural. God is very clear about not pulling up people who have passed on to talk to them.

What most people do not realize is that it is not really that person we are speaking with. It is a spirit in Satan's kingdom. Yes, a "familiar spirit" will know things about your child and emulate him or her to make you think you are speaking to your dead child. But you are giving yourself over to something even darker than the place you are already in. It might make you feel better emotionally for a few minutes; it may bring you some false comfort for a while, but no matter how much you want to believe it, the false is still false. And it will keep you going back to the darkness for false hope and false comfort.

Satan already does a good job of covering us with an evil blackness when our child leaves this earth. I refuse to live my life in his territory of darkness for a false hope and a false comfort of a spiritual entity pretending to be my child.

The best support is someone who knows you and will listen to you and be there with you—even better if they will cry with you. Someone you can share your fears and concerns with. Someone who will allow you to say and feel irrational things at times (but not let you hurt yourself in the process). If you are like I was, and don't know anyone who has experienced the death of a child, ask God to direct you to someone who seems genuinely concerned. Then let that person know you are looking for someone who cares to be a listener to all your emotions when you need to get them out. Not someone who will tell you how you should or should not be acting. (Another bereaved parent will not do that to you, as they know better from experience.) Someone who will hurt when you hurt and allow the pain to spill out, which helps work your way toward the healing you need.

One year after Becca's death, I was with a friend I only get to see once or twice a year at the most. She took me out for coffee and just let me share my heart and cry about Becca. One thing I shared with her is how horrible I felt that I was looking forward to going to heaven to see my daughter more than to see Jesus. Her response? "But, Laura, you've made a deposit!"

That, my friends, is the kind of support we all need! If you don't have it, ask God to bring it to you. He doesn't want you to stay in a place of darkness and hopelessness. He wants to use others in your life to bring healing. He already knows who He wants to send your way, so just ask, and keep asking until that person comes.

CHAPTER 5

||||||||||||||

The Bedroom of Rest

Don't *do*, just *be*.

This was the message I kept hearing from many different places for the first two years after Becca's leaving this earth. I believe it is a message we all need at some point when working our way through the darkness and back into the light.

A bedroom is part of our home where not many people are invited. It is a place of intimacy reserved just for ourselves and few others. We can't sleep or rest if there is a lot of activity surrounding us. We all need that place where we can go to get away and rest.

However, the rest we need to come into is not a time and a place. It is a position. But often we must begin with the time and place in order to learn to live in that position.

That means we have to set time aside specifically to be alone in God's presence. We need to "just be" in the stillness of His presence, where He can speak peace to us and fill us with His extravagant love, especially if we have a hard time believing He truly loves us after not stepping in to save our child from earthly death.

For me personally, over the years it has been easy to feel guilty in my quiet time with the Lord. I am either not following someone else's pattern, or I'm not doing what I have been told by other Christians I should be doing. I "should" be reading my Bible for thirty minutes every day, or I "should" be on my knees praying for an hour, etc.

But during this time of learning how to rest in God's presence, I was actually set free from that kind of guilt. In trying to "just be" with God, I never followed any kind of formula. If I wanted to pray, I prayed. If I wanted to sleep, I slept (usually with "soaking" music that would surround me with His presence). If I wanted to cry, I cried. If I wanted to praise Him with my voice or by lifting my hands, that's what I would do. If I wanted to spend time reading my Bible, I would open it and read. I learned to just have times of intimacy between myself and my Lord, and that has become a permanent part of my life.

I rest in the love of my God, and we spend time together, just the two of us in the privacy of my prayer room. I don't let what others do, or what others insist all Christians should do, dictate the intimate time set aside to be with my God, nor do I feel a need to tell others what they should be doing in their time of intimacy with Him.

Quiet Times with My God

So much depth and peace and revelation came out of those times of intimacy.

One day, while learning how to place myself in that position of rest, I had a deeper revelation of Romans 8:38-39:

> For I am persuaded that neither death nor life, nor angels nor principalities nor powers, nor things present nor things to come, nor height nor depth, nor any other created thing, shall be able to separate us from the love of God which is in Christ Jesus our Lord.

Even death cannot separate me from the deeply imbedded knowing that God loves me! And in that indescribable love, I can trust Him to do what is right and good for me, from His view, not mine. I can trust Him because I know Him and love Him and know without a doubt that He loves me even more. In my Bible I circled the word "Lord" and wrote, "That is the key—when we truly make him Lord, there is nothing that can pull us away from God's love!"

Here is a powerful revelation I received early in the process of learning how to fully enter into the rest of His love for me.

> 11/12/11: ...I was gripped by His holiness and was at His feet in the throne room. I heard Him shout out "My mercy covers this one!" It was like it rumbled out through all eternity into every kingdom—it was amazing, and I just sobbed. To know that God has declared me covered by the blood of Jesus, that the enemy has no hold on me, no right to me in any way... In my sin and humanity that He would love me so much that He took my place to pay for my sin, and His blood covers me so the enemy has nothing on me!

I can come under the blood of Jesus, and that's all I have to do! Rest in what was already done for me—truly amazing!

A few days later, I received the following revelation of a scripture that is often misunderstood. In Matthew 11:28-30 Jesus says,

> Come to Me, all you who are weary and burdened, and I will give you rest. Take My yoke upon you and learn from Me, for I am gentle and humble in heart, and you will find rest for your souls. For My yoke is easy and My burden is light. (NIV)

Let's read it in *The Message* version.

> Are you tired? Worn out? Burned out on religion? Come to me. Get away with me and you'll recover your life. I'll show you how to take a real rest. Walk with me and work with me— watch how I do it. Learn the unforced rhythms of grace. I won't lay anything heavy or ill-fitting on you. Keep company with me and you'll learn to live freely and lightly.

There are lots of theological teachings on what Jesus meant by this, including what it meant for Jesus, as a rabbi, to say this. But at this moment of my life, here is the revelation of what it meant to me.

> 11/29/11: Being yoked together with You is being yoked to that place of rest.

And here is how God actually began to apply that revelation to my life. Shortly after Becca died, I met a man named John Veal, whom God uses to speak into people's lives. As he began to pray over me, he reached up his hands and started brushing off my shoulders. He said God was showing him there was a heaviness on me, but it was not from anything I had done myself. It was from things that had been put on me. (He did not know me or anything about me.) He told me I needed to get away and go on a cruise. I chuckled, but he insisted that he was serious—that I needed to go away on a cruise. I had no intention of doing so, until later the subject came up again with someone else. I decided maybe I should look into this and brought it up to Dave. He is such an amazing and awesome man, agreeing it was a good idea to send me off on a trip where I could relax and process our daughter's death away from home. So six weeks after I buried my daughter, I went off by myself to the Caribbean for a five-day cruise.

12/4/11: Well, my adventure of "rest" has started! This will be the first trip where I don't have Becca's health on my mind. I know where she is and she is safe.... As I sit here writing, waiting for my plane to take off, I realize this is the first time ever in my life that I am going somewhere and absolutely no one is depending on me for *anything* and no one is expecting *anything* from me. I don't know what to think about that! How do I think? How do I act? This is going to be so very weird. Will I totally feel like a fish out of water? I'm having a hard time not tearing up just thinking about it.

Sitting on the front of the ship, waiting to pull out of port, I sat crying, texting Dave that I had no idea what I was going to do for five days. How do I do nothing? (And this man of whom I just said is so amazing and awesome was laughing at me hysterically, saying I am probably the only person who could be in tears about being on a vacation to do absolutely nothing.)

> 12/5/11: I am on my balcony getting ready for the ship to pull out. I can hardly stand this feeling of being cut off from everyone for four days! I was actually crying on the upper deck before I got my room. I feel so very alone and the tears are just running. Why is there such deep-rooted sadness and sorrow and pain? Where does it come from? And how am I supposed to get past it if I don't know the source?

I look at this now and see how ridiculous those questions are. But I was trying so hard to walk out my faith in victory (and didn't have anyone to help me sort out my confusion) that I couldn't see that this was a natural part of grieving, especially only being a few weeks out from my child's death.

The Holy Spirit continued to teach me about this place of rest that He wanted me to learn how to live from. He compared His love for me to a waterfall, how it would come down and drench me in His love. Later, a popular Christian song came out about that very thing. He would take me to the Song of Solomon and sweep me away in His love. I especially loved chapter 8, verse 5 that asks, "Who is this coming up from the wilderness leaning upon her beloved?"

While on the cruise I decided to allow myself to have some fun and rode a Segway.

In God's Schoolroom of Rest

Here are some conversations between me and my Beloved during that time as I struggled to learn how to live from a place of rest.

6/11/12: Help me to look to You in my times of brokenness and not to the wounds or the cause of the wounds. It's like being in a pit. It does not matter how I got into that pit, as far as You wanting to be my Shepherd, to get me out. I have two choices. I can either try to climb and crawl my way out, or I can call for You to come and carry me out.... I don't want to pretend like I have it all together. I don't want to just say that like good Christians are supposed to say! I want to be free to show that I am broken and yet You love me! But there have been times that openness has hurt me and been used against me… Is it okay to be open about being broken? We all are…even if there are people who turn my brokenness against me, I still want to be teachable in this; I want to learn how to love others in their brokenness.

My child, that is exactly what I am doing, and believe it or not, you are being a star student. You are getting an "A" in My book. No, you are not completely there yet, but when a teacher gives a grade, it is based on the material taught and covered—how well that student learned up to that point—and you are learning well. Keep up the good work—yes, I know you didn't want to write that, but do

you not admit that you have had to work at leaning on Me
and depending on Me to see you through this? It is work to
enter into My rest… so good work!

But am I truly resting in You? My mind
goes to my daughter so often!

You are in a process—remember slow and steady?
See it as the process it is, and allow Me to praise you and
love on you just like you started out asking for. See Me as
the Good Shepherd I am, loving on My little broken sheep!

Yes, I am beginning to see and understand
and am in awe of it. Brokenness is a gift. Only
when we know and admit how broken we are
can we truly experience the incredible depth of
Your love!

6/18/12: Father, my thoughts are all over
the place this morning…and most of it is based
on feelings. I don't feel strong, I don't feel like a
warrior, I don't feel joy…I used to absolutely love
having a busy life. I thrived on it, but now I just
don't want to do much of anything. I don't feel
like (there it is again) this is who I am supposed to
be, but I feel (again!) stuck in this place. I am not
in that black hole of depression, but I still am not
functioning in a normal way. What do I do?

Laura, you have heard Me speak to you several
times not to push yourself right now. There is a timing

and a purpose for this…don't try to force things right now, with things like fasting. You are still wounded. I don't have those kinds of expectations on you right now…all I have asked you to do is keep coming to Me, and you have. What you do with the rest of your time is pretty much up to you. Relax, read, sleep, go for walks, do a little work, you are okay. It is all okay…you are still having a hard time not "doing" and just "being" until I fully call you out of this place. I want you to enjoy this time without the blackness and depression and guilt! Don't make the mistake of pushing yourself and putting yourself on a schedule. Just enjoy being who you are and enjoy being free! I love you with a fierce love, and I am here for you, totally and completely. Just rest in My totally abandoned love for you, and don't think about, concern yourself with, or worry about anything else. Instead of feeling guilty about being free, you should be feeling guilty about trying to do what you think others think or expect you to do. Be free, My child! Be totally and completely free in Me!

7/31/12: Father, I want to thank You for how often I just feel content. I can't describe it, I can't put it into words, but so often throughout my days, I am surprised with a revelation at how content and at peace I am. That can only be You, and I want to take time specifically to thank You for that!

Laura, when you get thrown into the deep waters, there is turmoil and thrashing at the beginning. You either drown or you swim. You have learned to swim, but not only to swim, but to float in trust and rest. And it does not matter if the waters get deeper, because you are resting on top. Others around you can panic or try to help you, but you know—deep calls to deep. The deeper the waters, the more secure you are in your trust of Me. That is great faith! You asked Me for that years ago (yes, I remember, Lord) *so I have been at work to answer that prayer...*

This is not to say at some point I got it all figured out and now continually live from a place of rest. You see, what I have not shared with you yet is the other domino effect of Becca's death.

Because of Becca's severe heart illness, my son-in-law and I had ten years to grow an unusually close and loving relationship. But upon finding himself a widower, he admits he did pretty much everything they say not to do in the early period of grieving. Within weeks he got rid of their dog and moved out of their house, and within a few short months he started dating. As "mom," I was having a hard time watching these things happen, and a couple of times I tried to share with him some of my concerns. This caused him to put up a wall between us.

Apparently, at the same time, my nine-year-old granddaughter—who was having a difficult time with all these changes—would say things to him like "You're a bad dad." I guess he most often heard that when taking her home from spending time with us, but we were not aware of this. He assumed we were feeding this idea to her, and one day I received a message saying they were pulling out of our lives and we would not be seeing him or our granddaughter anymore. He refused to talk to us to work anything out and made it very clear that we were to leave them completely alone, with no contact whatsoever.

The pain was almost more than I could bear. Our granddaughter was an incredible blessing left behind by our daughter—a connection to her still on earth, and our legacy. We needed her and she needed us.

We began to learn that this is a somewhat common reaction to the in-laws when someone loses a spouse. I guess maybe they just want to move on with their lives, and staying in relationship with the previous in-laws makes them feel like they won't be able to do that.

We found out our state actually has a law against this very thing because it is such a common problem. We did not want to have to hire a lawyer to see our granddaughter; we wanted it done scripturally by sitting down with each other and working it out. We would let a few months go by and then try to contact him (including when her birthday came around), but he would get angry with us, making it clear he wanted nothing to do with us and refusing to allow us to see his daughter.

We found out at times he was tossing Becca's things. The pain of knowing there were specific items of my daughter's that I wanted, which now meant nothing to him, was enough to make me sob for hours. I just kept trying to tell myself, "It's just stuff…" But that only helped a little bit.

After almost a year of this, Dave sat down and wrote him a letter, explaining how we were still her grandparents, how the law was on our side, and if he would not sit down and talk with us (we were willing to do so with his pastor present), we would enforce our legal rights.

A few days before the given deadline, he agreed to meet with us, along with his new wife and their pastor, to at least talk about what had happened. God graciously entered that meeting, and we were able to forgive each other and open up the needed communication to start spending time with our granddaughter again.

During this time, God gave me many reminders to rest in Him and His ways. It was a hard thing to do, because I could not see any light in my darkness or understand why God was allowing so much intense pain.

He would share His reminders to just "be" and rest in Him in so many different ways. He would remind me to take a breath and breathe in His love and peace. He never sugarcoated anything but would acknowledge how difficult and steep my climb was, telling me to cling tightly to His hand, reminding me to look at Him whenever my circumstances overwhelmed me.

Anytime I felt like I was sinking under the swirling waters, I could call out "Lord, save me!" just like Peter did in Matthew 14, and somehow Jesus always reached through the storm and pulled me up out of the drowning sea of emotions, into His secure arms. He knew how weak and helpless I was, and He never tired of meeting me in my place of need. Looking back, I see now how each time He would free me from a few more of my shackles, even though most of the time I couldn't feel it.

Not only would He "hold" me, but He would encourage me to relax in the awareness of His presence. Some of my most precious times with the Lord were in my greatest times of weakness, just letting everything go and melting into His peace, love, and compassion.

During one of those times, I wrote in the margins of a devotional book I was reading, "Thank you! You know how utterly horrible the last two days have been, with total silence about seeing _____ (my granddaughter) for her birthday!"

I wish God would just speak a command and make it all better, taking away the pain and replacing it with constant peace

and rest, but it hasn't happened that way. Learning how to live
in that place has been a process.

> 6/13/12: I realized this morning with
> tears that while I have learned to accept the trials
> of this life, I have not gotten to the place where
> I can say I embrace them and love being broken
> because of the good that has come of it in my life.
> Holy Spirit, help me to get to that point. Show
> me, what are the incredible good things that have
> happened because of all these trials and times of
> deep brokenness?

At that point I wrote a list of eighteen things that God
has been able to work in me through the darkness, such as being
nonjudgmental, being broken, seeing the love and grace of
God in a deep way, becoming free of what man thinks of me,
enjoying being in His presence—just resting and letting Him
love on me, learning it's okay to be broken and to be a Christian
and a leader, etc.

> 4/21/13: This morning I just had to
> get to my prayer room, and there's been such a
> sweetness of just wanting to be here with Him. I
> finally put my finger on it: it is the contentment
> of surrender! I almost feel guilty for not being
> agitated or in some sort of emotional pain, but
> there is such a peace and contentment—very
> unnatural, and yet it should be natural, and I
> pray it has become a natural part of my life! I
> was just thinking that I am truly starting to learn

to live from the spiritual part of my being—Christ in me and I in Him—and not out of my emotions or flesh. I always thought I did pretty good at that, but I think the difference is walking in obedience and actually living it by tapping into who God is in me!

Let me say here, though, that the pain is still pretty intense at times, and I can feel like I am going backwards as I lose that peace and the place of rest I am fighting to keep.

For instance, during the writing of this book, my son-in-law dropped off four plastic tubs on our front porch. They were full of things he no longer wanted taking up space in his garage. Two bins held Becca's collection of Snow Buddies she put out every Christmas. One had all of her cassette tapes and CDs, and one contained lots of odds and ends, such as medical items used during her last year and a half of life, and some beautiful photo scrapbooks Becca spent hours on, including her wedding album and one of our granddaughter's birth and first few years of life.

But the thing that left me in a crying mess for the next few days was when I discovered her wedding dress smashed in the bottom of that bin. My heart still hurts, thinking about it. It felt so cruel, so careless, like she was no longer wanted or to be remembered. *My daughter's life has been reduced to four plastic bins,* I thought. Instead of allowing myself to go in that direction, I told myself the truth. Her life was much bigger than these four bins. However, it was another door of finality I had to painfully work through, and once again make a conscious decision to rest in who God is within the circumstance.

Becca's wedding day

Peace and Pain

It has now been well over three years since Becca graduated to her eternal home ahead of me, and the Holy Spirit is still teaching me how to stay in that place of rest. I wish I could say being rooted in a place of rest is now a way of life, but the truth is I am not there yet. I am still in the process.

One thing I am learning is that peace and pain can both reside in us at the same time. The pain of losing our child seems always to be there. As a parent dealing with the death of your child, I think you will understand what I mean when I say even if I'm not emotionally feeling the pain at the moment, it is still there. It's almost like a physical chronic pain. There are times you are so used to having the pain you don't even realize you're feeling it. Whether I notice the pain or not, an underlying peace seems to travel side-by-side with my pain. It is definitely the peace of God that goes beyond any understanding, and I am so thankful that He offers it to us and gives it freely.

Learning to rest in God is a must if you want to get out of your place of darkness. And that means spending time alone with Him. You don't even have to talk to Him, just "be" with Him. Don't feel guilty about taking time to be intimate with the One who loves you like crazy and wants to get you out of the pit and onto the path of living again. Spend intimate time with Him. Lots of it. Let Him show you the way out by showing you the fullness of Himself.

CHAPTER 6

||||||||||||

The Personal Care Room

I figure if God keeps my tears in a bottle (Psalm 56:8), I must have one of the biggest bottles in heaven!

I heard someone compare the pain of the death of a child as the opposite equivalent to the joy we felt the first day we held our baby on birthing day. Maybe it's because it has been almost twenty years since I experienced that awe of miraculous joy, but to me, if it were to be put on a scale of one to ten, comparing it with the joy of holding that child at birth, I would give it about a minus ten. The pain of the ending of that life feels so much greater to me than the joy of the entering.

When I think back to how I initially dealt with the pain, I realize I did a lot of poor eating and a lot of sleeping—not a very good combination, which has left me struggling with an extra thirty pounds or so.

I made so many excuses (to myself) for my food choices. Sweets became my comfort. And I slept for hours. Sleep was definitely my friend. As long as I was sleeping I could avoid the pain. Plus I think the pain was so intense that sleep was my body's defense mechanism to handle it.

I know the last thing you want right now is to be "lectured' in your time of tragedy, and that is definitely not my purpose. But because I care, and I don't want you to struggle as much as I did, I need to ask: how healthily are you eating, and are you getting any exercise?

The lack of taking care of my body has been a huge struggle, and still is. I have tried so many ways to motivate myself and keep myself on track. It's a hard uphill battle. As I am writing this, I'm finally getting a bit more consistent in eating what is good for me, allowing myself to get to the point where I crave what is healthy instead of what is unhealthy. I'm sad to say it has taken me almost five years to get to this point. (My terrible eating with "good" excuses started when Becca was in and out of the hospital her last eighteen months.)

Anniversary dates, birthdays, and holidays can be especially difficult in all areas, including this one of taking care of our bodies.

Giving God My Measuring Stick

For several years prior to Becca's passing, I had a yearly commitment to be in North Dakota the first week of October. I was returning from this yearly trip the night we lost Becca. The following year I decided to go ahead and make the trip again, knowing I would be home a couple of days before the one-year date of October 12.

What I didn't expect was how extremely difficult it was to be there. My thoughts kept turning to how clueless I was the year before, not knowing what I was about to go home and face.

> 10/8/12: So today at Bethel Church it hit me really hard about Becca—last year being there and the ministry and prayer that happened on her behalf that I thought was to be a part of her healing, having no idea how close her leaving was. I ended up going outside for quite a while, talking with Him about all of this...

I have a full page of what I wrote, but I'm going to keep that to myself. The following day, I made the twelve-hour drive home. At one of my stops I wrote the following:

> On the CFNI (Christ for the Nations Institute) CD *Desperate Hour*, the song "Overwhelmed" came on—it's one Becca and I sang together. And for the first time not just my head, but my heart was actually happy for Becca to be with Jesus, being overwhelmed by His beauty and majesty. But I've still been doing a lot of crying while driving. Time to get back on the road.

I didn't record anything else until October 14. I talk about how I went to an important family football game, but I couldn't stay. I kept thinking about what was happening exactly a year ago from that time, and the tears just kept running. And how the day before I fell apart completely and was pretty hard on myself. God was very gracious, telling me to quit judging myself because He was the judge of what was in my heart, and was not in judgment of me.

He made me give Him my "measuring stick" so I would quit judging myself by a standard He Himself was not using on me.

One month later I took a ministry trip to Uganda. It was by far the most stressful international trip I had ever been on because of several difficult circumstances with two of my hosts. I got back to the States the day before Thanksgiving and jumped right into the holidays. I thought the way I was dragging and literally barely able to function was a result of the stressful trip and not having a chance to get over jetlag. But it continued on past the holidays and well into January.

Several months earlier, I had started seeing a muscle response tester on a regular basis but had not had an appointment since right before my trip. When I finally arranged an appointment with her, she was extremely alarmed and told me she would not see me anymore until I went to a doctor. My body indicated that I was in severe adrenal fatigue and my organs were starting to shut down.

I was blessed to find a doctor who deals with natural methods of healing the body ahead of manmade solutions. Under his regimen, I was not allowed to take any trips and had to do everything I possibly could to go to bed early and sleep in late, to eat better, and to do as little as possible, which meant taking care of myself ahead of taking care of my family. I wasn't even supposed to exercise. I had been under so many years of stress (that go beyond losing Becca and are not written about in this book) that my body couldn't handle pushing out the "fight or flight" chemicals any longer and was shutting down.

I felt so stupid and useless. I felt guilty for letting myself get this way, even though all the events that led up to this were things I had no choice in. They came into my life without any permission from me whatsoever!

My healing has been slow, but I thank God it has been steady. However, I have yet to get this extra weight off and be able to stick with anything that might work. I don't want to get caught up in fad diets; instead I have been trying to eat healthy. Some of the things I have started but not followed through on are juicing, the Daniel fast way of eating, and low carbs in a healthy way.

Where am I with exercise? Well, I find myself caught in the circle of needing energy to do anything, but being told that in order to get that energy I must get out there and do something! I start doing daily walks (for maybe three or four days) and then quit. I do the same with my air stepper, biking, and other things.

Within this struggle, though, I have hope. Why? Because I care and I am trying. I'm aware and I'm taking steps—baby ones, but steps to becoming more healthy in my eating and getting more active.

I am also learning how much of a healthy lifestyle is based on my perspective. I can either treat myself to that piece of cake, to that pan of brownies, to those marshmallows...you get the point...or I can choose to "treat myself" to something healthy.

Physically, it is just as easy for me to choose some organic peanut butter with veggies or an apple as it is for me to choose a couple of handfuls of sugary cereal. It is all in the perspective of my mindset.

Even though I've gotten much better since my adrenal fatigue diagnosis, I can still feel my limitations more than I want to. And it rears its ugly head at times in a strong way. It kicks in sometimes while writing this book, because writing immerses me back into the emotions of such a painful part of my life. At times I've had to put this project aside and just "be" in a place of rest.

For the most part, adrenal fatigue has actually been a good thing for me. It has forced me to slow down and enjoy life. I used to be a person who crammed my life so full that I was constantly going from one thing to another without much downtime at all, or time set aside to make fun moments with the family. While I am still working toward my complete healing, I don't ever want to go back to being that person again. I know I missed out on things in Becca's life along with my other children because I was always so busy. I can never get that time back, but I can keep myself from becoming that person again and continue missing out on my children and grandchildren. This past Valentine's Day I had an all-out party for our grandkids. It was so much fun we decided to make it a yearly tradition.

Just One Thing at a Time

Before ending this chapter, I want to turn a corner and say something about our thoughts and how our mind operates during extreme bereavement. I became so forgetful it drove me crazy. I would get so frustrated with myself at the things I would forget, at the things I didn't or couldn't remember, at my constant confusion and fuzziness. It took me quite a while to find out that was a normal part of intense grief.

I started speaking over myself according to 1 Corinthians 2:16 ("I have the mind of Christ") and 2 Timothy 1:7 ("I have a sound mind"). Eventually the fog began to clear and I wasn't quite so scattered and forgetful. After three years, I have to be honest and say I still don't have a clear mind like I did before. It can be very frustrating at times. Friends have tried to encourage me by saying things like "Oh, I forget things too." But this isn't the same thing as just getting forgetful with age. We have been through a traumatic event, and our minds just freeze, forgetting how to function at times. I keep giving it to God and don't allow myself to be stressed out about it.

What was happening with me physically and in my mind during the worst of my grieving period those first couple of years seemed so much greater than my strength to get through it. In a very real sense, the mental and emotional "energy" of grief saps brain power and leaves a person quite disoriented and unable to hold a thought for very long.

There are those who would tell us it is our choice to either lean on God for strength or fall apart, but that wasn't the case for me. I did both. I leaned on God as I fell apart. Only those who have lost a child can understand there are times when the intense grief of those first few months and years will emotionally and physically take over, and we really have no choice in the matter. We can't function no matter how much we try or how much we might want to. On those days I would cry out to God. It was the *only* thing I could do. And in that place of trauma, God has never rejected me. I still occasionally have times like this, and I can still call out to Him with the tiniest cry at *any* point, and He comes in to give me the strength I need, moment by moment, until I can function again.

Don't you love it when people become our cheerleaders, telling us we can do this because we are such a strong person? Or when someone tells us they admire us for how strong we are? Or that they could never go through what we are going through in losing a child. WHAT? News flash: we had no choice in the matter! We are being *forced* to go through this. And just because you see us in survival mode doesn't mean we are being strong.

We need to find ways beyond just the spiritual to bring ourselves comfort in our time of grief, and it is very easy to do so in unhealthy and even harmful ways. Doing things to numb ourselves from the pain will only prolong the grief and even intensify it. Obviously, we know the dangers of excessive drugs and alcohol, but there are lots of things we can do excessively that are not good for us. Things like excessive shopping, excessive Internet or TV, and excessive eating or sleeping. Sometimes we may do some of these things because we just need to shut down for a while. And that is okay! But we want to monitor ourselves to make sure it is not a substitute for going to God to help us get through this.

One thing God so graciously shared with me in all my times of sleeping was the reminder that He never sleeps or slumbers. He could still minister to me while I was sleeping. And He can and wants to do the same thing for you. Ask Him to bring healing to your soul while you are sleeping. He doesn't need us to be awake.

Here is the last thing I want to encourage you with in this chapter of rest. This is a process! It takes time. Do the next thing you can do, whatever it is, no matter how small it is—that's it. Just one thing at a time. Don't try to look too far ahead. It is exhausting and overwhelming. You have permission to give yourself lots and lots of grace, especially when others do not!

CHAPTER 7

||||||||||||||

The Kitchen of Usefulness

Years ago I used to comfort myself in hard times with the thought *at least one pain I've never had to deal with is losing a child.* Obviously, that is no longer true.

Even in the deep pain of this new trial I never wanted to experience (none of us do), I made myself available to God to do what He wanted with it. I told God He could use me for others with this pain, and He said, *"I don't want to USE you—I want to LOVE you! I will use your circumstances, but I won't use you like that!"*

What a precious thing for God to tell me at that time. He will never use any of us for His agenda in the way that people use and take advantage of each other. That was a pretty deep revelation for me.

All kinds of good and useful things happen in a kitchen, such as lots of cooking, baking, eating, laughter, and talks. I can't tell you how many times one of my kids has come to talk to me in the kitchen, and we ended up sitting on the counters or the floor as the discussion went way beyond the time being used to do whatever it was I was doing in that room.

Because the kitchen is such a busy place, there is a lot of cleaning that goes on in there as well. The kitchen is often the most used room in a house. It can be a wonderful place of gathering, but it can also be a place of isolation, as someone prepares food or cleans while the rest of the family is in a different room.

We know Satan is a roaring lion. We know he is a devouring wolf. And we are sheep. Those who hang on the outer fringes of the flock or wander and go their own way are the first ones the enemy will pick off. They are easy prey. So the enemy will go out of his way to plant thoughts in our minds and make us believe we have good reasons to isolate ourselves.

The death of a child is one he loves to amplify. We've already been messed with because of how painful and unnatural and just plain wrong it is to bury our child! And now he comes along and uses that intense pain to prompt us to isolate ourselves.

Doing vs. Being

Before I continue, I want to differentiate something here. All my life I've been a doer. I did not know how to just be. I was a people pleaser, and doing things gave me my sense of value and importance. So yes, I did need to learn how to see myself the way God sees me—that my value and importance come from just being who I am. But there is a difference between learning this with the Holy Spirit as your teacher, in His time and His way, as opposed to this lesson being forced on you by someone.

When my pastor put me in a place of "rest" and isolation, it went on for weeks and then months. I don't even remember how long my husband had off from work, but at some point he went back. About a week after the funeral, my youngest son went back to school. The rest of the kids also got back to their previous life schedules. Were they all in a fog? No doubt about it. But even going through the motions of life helped them. I didn't have that.

I would spend hours and hours in my prayer room, mostly sleeping and crying. I would read my Bible, pray for a while, cry, and then sleep some more. That became my life because I had nothing to go back to, since my pastor would not allow me to have any kind of ministry or leadership role in the church.

Just today, one of my granddaughters came into my prayer room, saw my sleeping bag on the floor, and asked me, "Grandma, do you sleep in here sometimes?" I told her not as much as I used to, and that I slept here a lot when Becca died. Immediately tears welled up in my eyes as I remembered this time of painful isolation that was forced on me for months.

Here is something from my journal that shows you how much it was messing with me emotionally.

1/22/12: God, I feel like the most immature Christian on the face of the earth! How can You possibly use me for Your glory or move through me? I am a basket case of emotions... I am broken and useless, and I seem to have it in my face that I am not someone You can flow through. It's about You—it's not about me—but then why did You create me? Why would You even want me? I am such a failure. I can't figure out who I am or what I am supposed to be or do. I am not consistent in anything in my life. I live by my emotions and can't seem to walk in Your

Spirit instead of my own flesh! Just the fact that I am in such discouragement shows what a failure I am in this life!

God PLEASE, PLEASE get me to the place where all I need is You! The only thing that matters in my life is You! That's just another sign of my immaturity and being a failure! Why aren't You enough?

How do I get to the place where I don't care how anyone treats me, I don't care what anyone thinks about me, I don't care that I am taken advantage of, I don't care if I am special or important to anyone? The place where You are all I need and everything is fine and dandy because I am complete in You? Every single thought that has gone through my head for the last four hours just confirms how badly I have failed—in my walk with the Lord, with my family, with my life. Yes, God is faithful, yes, He has never failed me— which means it is ALL ME!

I continued this way for several more lines and ended with the questions:

What do I do? How do I do it? How do I just "let go" so that nothing bothers me?

I have since come to believe I was crying out from a place of false teachings of what a strong and mature Christian looks like. First, that I should have my emotions under control at all times, and second, that I don't need anyone or anything except Christ. Maybe calling those two things false teachings is a bit harsh. But we hear words that make us think these things, both in our worship songs and from the pulpit. Words that tell us we should be able to live our lives not needing anybody or anything except Jesus, and the only emotion we should have is rejoicing in His goodness. But the truth is, many scriptures express the strong negative emotions of those who loved God, especially David in the book of Psalms. And a lot of scriptures talk about coming into unity with each other and needing each other in the body of Christ. I need you and you need me. God created us to need each other.

I have no problem submitting to the leaders God has placed over me. But something is very wrong when a spiritual leader becomes the voice of the Holy Spirit in a person's life, and when that leader tries to override a woman's husband as her covering. But during this time of intense grief, I allowed both of those things to happen, and it nearly destroyed me.

Dave kept asking me, "When is this time of rest supposed to be over?" All I could tell him was that I didn't know. Although he wholeheartedly welcomed my season of rest after Becca's passing—even sending me on a cruise to relax and enjoy myself—when the weeks turned into months and he saw me spiraling even further into despair, he became very concerned. He saw how wrong it was for me to be kept in this prolonged place of "rest", knowing I needed to return to the things God had called and anointed me to do in ministry, which would allow the Holy Spirit to flow through me to others as part of my healing.

The Gift of Participation

As I started reading books and joining Facebook groups, I kept hearing from other grieving parents how having something to do, like a job or some sort of responsibility, was a huge gift. It allowed them to be able to function again. I'm not talking about "busy work" to avoid the pain of processing what happened, but doing something that caused at least one shattered piece of their life to feel normal again. They might have been in a fog, they might not remember any of it, but at least it kept them from sitting around with nothing but their thoughts taking them deeper and deeper into depression.

There actually was one area I still functioned in. The international ministry I was a part of had a correspondence school, and I was the administrator of that school. I have no idea how I did it, but somehow I limped my way through overseeing the students. But there were things that definitely fell through the cracks, and students did not have much of my attention beyond just grading their work. My leader, Becky Fischer, was full of grace and did not pull me from my job, allowing me to work in a state of barely functioning. I honestly don't believe I would even be alive today if I did not have that job and those students as a thin connection to my previous world beyond my isolated grief.

I am telling you all this because I don't want you to do to yourself what was done to me. God can still minister through you and use your circumstance *while* you are broken and working through your grief. In fact, I believe that in a rather short amount of time you *need* to allow yourself to be a vessel God can flow through.

When we have nothing in ourselves to give, God seems to flow in a very strong way through us. We are completely out of His way and we find 2 Corinthians 12:10 being fulfilled in our lives: when we are weak, He is strong through us. Feeling His strength flow through our weakness and our brokenness stirs life and brings some of that deep healing we need in our souls.

Eventually, God led us to a church that is nonjudgmental and full of God's love and grace. I am back to having the Holy Spirit flow through me on a worship team. And there are still times when I am up front facing a room full of people, singing into a microphone with tears running down my face.

I can 100 percent guarantee you're not going to feel like participating at first. You might even cry while you're doing it (whatever "it" is). That's okay. The important thing is to allow God to use your circumstance to touch others, and let Him flow through you as soon as possible.

Don't wait until you feel strong. God is so gracious, so faithful, so deeply in love with you and full of compassion for you. He knows exactly what will bring a healing touch to your innermost being. So when an opportunity comes your way, whether it is public like my being on the worship team, or private such as someone asking you to connect with a friend of theirs who just lost a child, I encourage you to make yourself push through and do that one thing. Then push through and do the next thing that comes your way.

Have someone compassionate and caring pray for you, to give you the strength and whatever else you need to follow through. Remember, when we are weak He is strong. And based on how deep our weakness is as a grieving parent, that is a very powerful strength He has for each of us!

One of my favorite pictures of Becca and me, taken after her stroke

CHAPTER 8

||||||||||||||

Looking Out the Window of Fear

Fear brings torment, and as parents grieving the earthly loss of our child, it is easy to feel the full weight of that torment. What are some of those fears?

- That going forward with your life will cause those around you to forget your child ever lived
- That there will be moments when you don't think about or even miss your child
- That laughing or having fun without your child means you're a bad parent
- That you may lose your other children, making it hard to let them go (either out of your sight or to grow up and be on their own)
- That your child may not be in heaven

If we are afraid of something, it means that thing has more power over us than we do over it. So if we are afraid to face the pain of our grief and work our way through it, our fear will continue to control us. I don't believe this is what you want or you would have quit reading this book by now.

There is something much more powerful than our deepest fears: God's love for us! God's perfect love casts out all fear (1 John 4:18). If we have fear, it is because we don't believe in His perfect love for us. And that's understandable, because it is hard to reconcile in our minds how we can trust a God who says He loves us and yet allowed this terrible thing to happen to our child and to us.

I can offer no easy fix or solution to this, although it is very black-and-white. We either believe God is good and Satan is evil or we don't. We either fear that God isn't big enough or we have faith that He is more than enough.

If I can make God do whatever I want Him to do, including stepping in to stop the death of my child, then He is no longer God. He then becomes a magic genie in a bottle that we can rub and have Him make our wishes come true. I don't want a God who is limited to what people tell Him to do. I want a God who is bigger and mightier than that. I want a God who is so big our minds cannot comprehend who He is and what He does and how He does it.

I choose to live my life with faith in that kind of a God, a God whose love is perfect, going beyond what my mind can make sense of. And because He loves with a perfect love, I don't have to walk in *any* fear because He is with me, and I know someday I will get to see the whole picture I am blinded to right now.

And that is how the fear of not knowing whether or not your child is in heaven can be tamed. God's love for your child supersedes your love for him or her. Each one of us is created with His desire to have an intimate relationship with us, not just here on earth, but for all of eternity. I believe God is big enough to have made every opportunity possible for your child to accept Him before leaving this earth. This could easily have happened during a time you know nothing about (including crying out to Him at the moment of death). So give that fear to God, trusting that He took care of it. Not having the information you want to have doesn't mean it did not happen at some point in their lives.

Making a Shift in How You See God

After addressing that specific fear, I now want to share with you a few things to help make a shift in how you see God in the midst of any other fear caused by the pain of your tragedy.

1. Some parents are helped by the realization that their child is not missing; he or she is simply absent.

   To be absent means not to be present for the moment. The Bible says that for someone who has accepted the gift of salvation, to be absent from the body is to be present with the Lord (2 Corinthians 5:8). I have used a term in this book that some bereaved parents don't like—the idea of "losing" our child. They will say they have not lost their child because they know exactly where that child is. I understand what they are saying; however, I have lost my child from this earth. She is now absent from my presence for the rest of my time here on earth.

This is one of those times where perspective can change everything. I can either focus on my personal loss that my child is permanently absent from this earth, or I can focus on the fact that my child is absent from this earth but present with the Lord, and even though the pain is intense, I will meet up with my child again in our eternal home, never to be separated again. It may not seem like it, but our perspective is a choice we make. I strongly recommend you choose the second perspective, saving yourself lots of torment.

2. Being able to take my needs and my fears to God in prayer makes a big difference in my life.

   It keeps me from feeling so helpless in a circumstance I have no control over. Praying gives me much more control over how I respond to my feelings and fears. It may be that the only thing I have control over is my communication with God, but that is actually enough.

   I think of Peter's answer when Jesus asked His twelve followers, "Will you leave Me also?" Peter said, "Lord, who else can we go to? You have words that give life that lasts forever" (John 6:68 NLV). For many years I have said Jesus isn't a crutch to me. He is my wheelchair. That is truer now than it has ever been.

3. Having the revelation that God *always* leads us into triumph makes a huge dent in our fears.

During a worship song at church one day, I suddenly realized that if I bring God into my battle (including the battle of my fears and my darkness) then I will win, because it is impossible for Him to lose! He is the Alpha and Omega, the beginning and the end. God has the first and last word in my life, and He also has it in the life of my child! God has never entered a battle where He came out as the loser, and He never will. As soon as I ask God to fight for me, I know somehow in the end I will come out victorious!

4. Reading the book of Psalms in the Bible can be extremely helpful.

Over and over the writer cries out for help from a very dark place of despair. And God responds by being a rock, a refuge and help in times of need. I spend a lot of time there when I "relapse" and find myself struggling with the pain and reality that Becca is gone and I won't see her again until I join her in heaven.

5. Don't keep looking back, allowing yourself to be paralyzed by the pain of the past, trying to stay in a place which no longer exists. I am so sorry to say this, and I am not trying to be cruel, but simply want to set you free; no matter how much you want your child's life back, it isn't going to happen. I did that, and here is what God spoke to me one day.

12/31/12: Laura, DON'T LOOK BACK! Go forward with everything you've got! Lot's wife looked back and she was frozen to a place where she died. She could not go anywhere because she looked back. I know that may seem harsh, but it will become a tormenting fear that will paralyze you. Don't look back at the crushing blow; if you look back to ponder and relive the death, you won't be able to walk in the power of My resurrection life. LIVE! You shall live and not die! I speak over you, my daughter, that you shall LIVE and not die! I speak life into your soul, into your very being—LIFE! Receive it! Just receive this new life I am giving you. You will grow stronger in it each day you come up to Me to drink. Drink daily. Drink deeply. For it will truly be a wellspring of life in you and through you. Cross over from death to life! Cross over from sorrow into joy! Cross over into new depths of My love and My will and My ways for your life.

6. Don't try to hide from your fears or pretend they aren't there.

God wants you to bring all your feelings to Him, even the ones you wish you didn't have. You may be wondering, *He knows these things already. Why should I have to tell Him how I am feeling?* Because you need to admit those things so you can give them to God and let Him work with you at being set free. Fear and anxiety come from the enemy of your soul. When you take these feelings to God, it is a way of affirming your trust in Him, regardless of how you feel. If you do this persistently, those tormenting feelings of fear will eventually lose their hold on you, and you will find your feelings lining up with faith.

7. Claim the promises of God, not based on how you feel, but based on the truth of what God says.

I have chosen to believe Romans 8:18, which tells me the sufferings of this present time cannot be compared with the glory that will be revealed in me. And I have written in the margin of one of my Bibles that I am not waiting for the glory of heaven, but I am looking for the power of His glory to be revealed in me while I am still here on this earth!

How about the promise of Jesus telling us He will never leave us or forsake us (Hebrews 13:5)? That is not a promise based on conditions. It is set and firm, no matter what we choose to do or not do. He is our constant companion and source of everything we need during this time. The question is not "Where is God?" The question is "Where am I?" I can walk out on Him very easily, and many of us do. We ignore Him, as though He is no longer with us. That is never the case. Guess who moved away? (Hint: it's not God.)

Over the years, I have struggled with having enough faith to please my Father based on Hebrews 11:6, especially when I hear about people having gold dust on them, or feathers appearing, having open visions, seeing things like angels or a glory cloud, and so on.

One day I was crying, wanting to have the kind of faith that pleases Him, yet in such deep pain over the death of my daughter. Where was my faith? In the midst of all my tears, God kept telling me how much pleasure I bring Him *because* of my deep faith. He showed me His perspective: it is easy to believe and walk with Him when people see open visions or encounter Jesus in dreams (the way the heavens are open to a seer prophet). But it takes a lot more faith to keep on when a person doesn't see those things.

Great faith brings God great pleasure, and I was bringing Him great pleasure. As you keep on, trusting Him in your pain, even though you can't see where He is leading you in all this, you are bringing Him great pleasure as well.

What fears are you carrying right now? Are they things God would have you carry? Let me answer that for you. No, they are not. So are you willing to lay them down at the feet of Jesus, who is sitting on His throne as King, and leave them there so you can move forward in freedom?

There is freedom in surrender. I have experienced that in my life over and over again. It is like we are digging through the garbage, trying to survive, when God wants to hand us a steak. But we won't take it because we don't want to give up the garbage. Crazy, isn't it? But that is what we do when we refuse to allow God to take something like our fears from us. He always replaces it with something better. If you say yes and hand over those fears, God can move in and begin to turn things around for you. (Hmm…that makes me think of another promise you can claim in Romans 8:28.)

There are some things we need to give to God for Him to do, but there are also things we can do ourselves. Right now you can speak to the mountain of fear in your life. Tell the lies behind that fear that you are going to believe the truth: God's perfect love for you casts out *all* fear!

While writing this chapter, I found myself leaning back in my recliner and telling God out loud, "I am so very, very blessed!" How can I say that? Because I am! I refuse to remain focused on the pain of my loss. I am determined to go forward, focused on who and what I still have. I have given God the shattered pieces of my life and am watching Him not only fix it, but make it into something even more beautiful than it was before. Only a God who specializes in miracles can do that!

I also refuse to live in fear of the "what ifs" of more loss. If that happens, I know that *I know* that *I know* God will give me the grace I need to get through it. Why waste my time on the darkness of fearing what will probably never happen? I would much rather live my life full of light and hope of a better tomorrow, both here on earth and in my eternal home with Becca. You and I both are blessed with so much that has *not* been taken from us.

Fear and faith require the same emotion, which is belief in the unknown.

Which "unknown" are you going to believe in and act on? I recommend faith.

Glamor shot with my daughters

A family Christmas photo (before our fifth child)

CHAPTER 9

||||||||||||||

A Spiritual Fireside Chat

Something that amazed me after Becca died was how often the Word of God was exactly what I needed, and other times it was the wrong thing at the wrong time. For someone who has never gone through something like this, that may almost sound heretical.

Let me try to explain. Usually, when a well-meaning friend would quote a scripture at me, it was some "Christianese" generic answer to all of life's problems. It wasn't a verse given to them specifically by the Holy Spirit to share with me from God, something I needed for my broken soul at that exact moment.

When a scripture was thrown in my face to tell me what the Bible said I should be feeling or saying, or how I should be acting, it did more damage than good. But when I sat down and it was just me and God, He would lead me to the exact places in His Word to bring just what I needed for that moment.

Why, Lord?

Most grieving parents will question "Why?" And some will turn a corner and become okay with not knowing why. In order to go forward, we find we must choose to trust and have faith in the only One who can answer that question, even when He doesn't answer it for us. How do we get past the whys? I don't believe there is a magical answer or a formula we can follow. Sorry. All I can say is we each have to come to the place where we become weary of asking why and accept that God sees the whole picture. And even if He did tell us why, it wouldn't really matter, would it? We are still without our child.

Have you ever known a child who was always asking why, not because he actually wanted to know why but because he wanted to be able to argue against your answer? Even if God told you why, would you be okay with it? In our deepest pain, I don't think we would. And so we have to get to the point where we quit wrestling with it and become like Jacob and say, "I'm not going to let go until you bless me through this! I'm not going to let this be wasted in my life, God. I am done asking why, and now I am going to ask how. How are You going to use this in my life?"

Even before Becca died, I would agree with Job in the Bible and tell God, "Even if You slay me, I will trust You and serve You" (Job 13:15). And I have continued through the tears and anguish to speak that out to Him and to myself. There are times it is not easy to say or feel, but I say it anyway. "God, even with my daughter being taken from me on this earth, I will trust You and serve You."

I would encourage you to make the same statement to God. You may ask, "How can I say that when I don't believe it?" I'm glad you asked. You can say that because it is true by faith. Remember when Jesus went to a girl who had died and was laughed at because He told the people she wasn't dead but was "sleeping" (Matthew 9:24)? There was no doubt she was dead. But Jesus was speaking by faith what He knew to be true.

Her spirit was not dead. He was calling her spirit back into her body to bring life back to her on this earth. Romans 4:17 says God "gives life to the dead and calls things which do not exist as though they did." That is what Jesus was doing. And that is what we can do also in Him.

So go ahead and say it. "It doesn't matter what happens to me on this earth. God, I will trust You, and I will serve You." You are speaking what does not exist, trusting that God has already done what needs to be done to make it true. I can guarantee it will break something off of you, because a freedom happens when we surrender completely to the God who loves us more than we could ever imagine. We *must* begin to look past our pain and trust His love for us.

For those of you who would like a scripture to meditate on to help you with this, turn to Habakkuk 3:17-18 (NLT):

> Even though the fig trees have no blossoms, and there are no grapes on the vines; even though the olive crop fails, and the fields lie empty and barren; even though the flocks die in the fields, and the cattle barns are empty, yet I will rejoice in the Lord! I will be joyful in the God of my salvation!

This passage gives me so much hope. I don't have to have the answers because I choose to trust the One who has them. And I trust that He is a good and perfect Father, and there is a reason He's not giving those answers to me. I choose to be okay with that, and I choose to rejoice in the Lord with whatever measure of energy or emotions I have for that moment. And, honestly, some days it is a lot while other days it's not much at all.

I have chosen to trust and believe He is good, all the time. He isn't just good when things are going my way. He isn't my servant who will do what I want at the ring of a bell. My God is bigger than any man, bigger than any tragedy. And when I need to, I will follow the simple instructions of Psalm 46:10. I will quiet myself before Him, and be still and know that He is God (and I am not).

The enemy wants us to believe we are alone, but that is a lie. God will *never* leave us and *never* forsake us. You may be thinking, *If that's true, why did He let my child die? He did leave me. He did forsake me.*

Many grieving Christian parents go through a time where they get angry with God and turn their backs on Him. They can't believe in a God who would take their child from them. But Jesus warned us we would have tribulation in this world (John 16:33).

Here is one of my struggles with anger and frustration taken from my journal.

6/26/13: Holy Spirit, why the despair? Why the weeping? Why the anger? For days now...why? What is going on internally that is causing all of this? I throw myself at Your mercy and cry out HELP ME! And I'm so angry that I am even struggling like this! I feel so fake! How can I be a Spirit-filled Christian and be struggling like this? How can I spend time with You for hours in some seasons and be like this? How can I be putting this prayer room to so much use and be so much in my flesh?

I knew better than to blame God, but as you can see, I was fighting it. We have to realize that God is not the cause of death; the enemy is.

Yes, God could have stepped in and saved our child, and that is beyond what I can understand. I have a finite mind. I don't know why He didn't save Becca, and I don't know why He didn't save your child. But what I do know is **there is no greater time for our need to have God at work in our lives than the death of our child.** Without God there is no hope. And without hope, we will be stuck in our pit of despair. It is impossible to be neutral. We either move toward God, or we move away from Him. But when we move away from God, we are moving away from the One who can give us the greatest strength possible to get through this.

God did not leave me. He carried me through it. I can't say He walked with me—I don't think I did much walking for quite some time. As I already said, God is not my crutch to prop me up; He's my wheelchair to carry me. And He certainly was during that painful dark time.

Zephaniah 3:17 has been one of my favorite verses for many years. It tells us God is in the midst of us, that He renews us in His love. And that He actually rejoices and dances over us with singing, which is an amazing thought to me. I have come to realize He isn't excited about me only when I'm happy, or only when I am excited about Him. There are no conditions or limitations to His excitement over me. As a matter of fact, my Bible tells me He is even closer to me when I am bruised and broken and have a crushed spirit (Psalm 34:18).

Many Christians have been taught that God has a wonderful plan for their lives. We think that means our life is going to be great—full of fun, laughter, sunshine—and nothing bad will ever touch us. But that is something man says. God never said He has a wonderful life for us here on earth. I already reminded us that Jesus said we will have hard times. Jesus said those who mourn will be comforted (not that we will never mourn). He said we will always have the poor with us (He didn't end poverty). These are the things He will use the most to draw us closer to Himself, to bring us to a place of being victorious. (How can you have a testimony without a test?)

Wonder and Goodness Ahead

God does have a plan for your life. It is full of wonder and amazement at the goodness and faithfulness of God, through both the incredible blessings and the painful tragedies. Through both, we have the opportunity to see His hand at work in our lives, to give Him the glory and the honor He so deserves.

The truly wonderful part happens when we leave this sinful world and move to eternity with Jesus. And just think, as a side note, we have someone very dear and close to us who has beat us there.

Here are some random nuggets I received and wrote down in those first couple of years that I would like to pass along to you before we leave our fireside chat.

- Somewhere I heard or read the words "Spiritual blessings come wrapped in trials." I wrote a note saying: "The loss of a child is an awfully deep trial to wrap a blessing in!" God's unexpected answer followed: *I know, because My Son died, and it was wrapped in the blessing of you!*
- "I am with you" is the parachute in my freefall.

- Just like crossing on a tightrope, don't look down; keep looking at the focal point—where I am going. Don't look down at the circumstances—stay focused on Jesus (the author and finisher of my faith!).
- You have to keep walking into His presence until you walk out of yourself!
- It is impossible for me to have a need God cannot meet
- *Everything* in our lives is redeemable (Isaiah 43:1): "Fear not, for I have redeemed you; I have called you by your name; you are Mine."
- God is an expert at bringing life from death.

A friend of mine lost her twenty-two-year-old son, Josh, in a car accident six months after we lost Becca. I love what she wrote and pray it blesses you:

> Do we sacrifice the joy of having children to spare us the pain that occurs if we lose them either by death or rebellion? I think not. The joy we receive from our children outweighs any pain from the loss. I would take my twenty-two years with Josh over and over again with the same outcome if that was the only way I would have the honor of being his mother.
>
> Going through all this has spread a little light onto why our Father in heaven would create this world and allow us to have our own free will. He knew we would rebel and He knew the only way to save us from ourselves would be to sacrifice Himself on our behalf. He also knew

the joy of creating us in His own image would outweigh that pain.

The love we feel for our children, as all-consuming as it seems, is only a speck of the love our God has for us.

Try to imagine that...it's impossible to comprehend.

—*Kathy Pelton*

CHAPTER 10

||||||||||||||||

Sitting on the Porch of Your Identity

Victim or victor? As grieving parents, which one are we?

My name, Laura, means victory or victorious spirit. That is who I am. My life has given me multiple opportunities to choose if I am going to be a victim or a victor. And by the grace of God, so far I had always triumphed in victory! But this situation was completely different from anything I had ever gone through. When it came to losing Becca from this earth, I realized it is not necessarily one or the other, always on top or always on the bottom. It is a process, a process that can take me back and forth between the two in any given second.

For many years my identity as a mom was tied to whatever difficult thing my children were going through. That sounds horrible, doesn't it? But it's true. I never would have admitted it, even to myself, until now. And it really escalated when Becca was in and out of the hospital for those last eighteen months. I was Becca's mom, and that is what made me special.

After Becca died it continued. There was so much self-pity. I wanted everybody to know how much pain I was in. I wanted people to be able to see it on me. I wanted people to feel sorry for me because I had gone through something far worse than anything they had ever experienced. My identity was being a grieving mom. Self-pity and allowing my identity to be that of a victim caused the black hole I was in to go even deeper.

As I was working on this very chapter, I took a break and ended up on Facebook. Someone had just posted a question asking how you can tell when you are turning that corner and things are starting to get better. Here is one of the answers given: "When you can introduce yourself without the urge to add 'and my daughter died' after your name." It is definitely something we do—the death of our child becomes our identity.

Victim No More

We all need to stop playing the victim card at some point. This is actually what could be called self-pity. It will send you even deeper into the pit you have found yourself thrown into. You have to get to the point where you want out more than you want to stay there, no longer wanting the death of your child to be the identity of who you are. You have to want to see the light of hope. The rays of this light can reach any depth. It usually starts with just a tiny dim ray. As you continue focusing on that small light, without even realizing it, the light will start to pull you up, until you can grab the hand of the giver of that Light and see His face.

The only way out is to change your identity. No one else can do that for you. And the first part of it is to admit that is where you are, and that you are there because you choose to be there. I am not saying you chose to be a parent who lost your child. What I am saying is that if your identity is being a parent who has lost your child, you are choosing to allow it to continue (even if it is only to yourself).

I really do understand it! We want to be identified as a victim of this horrible circumstance. But we have to ask ourselves: *am I going to choose to get my identity from the circumstance, or am I going to choose to get my identity from the truth of who I am and who I belong to?*

Since I have given my life to Jesus Christ, my true identity is a daughter of the Most High God. My Daddy and my King are who I chose to look up at from within my painful pit. Because I know my God, I knew that somehow, some way, He could pull me out, and I could once again walk in my true identity as His daughter, instead of wrapping myself up in the very dark identity of being a victim of the most tragic event possible on this earth.

> 12/6/11 *The victory is not in your winning battles, but in your knowing how loved and precious you are as My daughter, the beloved daughter of the Almighty God and King!*

Three months after Becca's death, I had the following revelation. This brought so much understanding to my grief as a mom that I can't even put it into words. It has been a *huge* part of my understanding why I am so very connected to my children, and why we as mothers feel the death of our child so deeply for the rest of our lives. My hope and prayer is that it does the same for you!

> 1/18/12: 1) I am a spiritual being in a physical body 2) I *do* feel much closer to the reality of heaven and that part of the spiritual realm now 3) death is a spiritual event, a crossing

over into the spirit realm. Because she is a part of me, it was within my womb that she received her spirit. (WHOA! Now there is a Selah! I was carrying her spirit within me as I carried her as a fetus!) The death of her body and the leaving of her spirit affect me in a way they affect no one else. Okay, Holy Spirit, you've got to show me some scriptures to base this on. It makes perfect sense, but I need to see confirmation in Your Word! That is why a mom's identity is wrapped up in her children!

God immediately gave me the following examples to confirm this revelation, which I also recorded.

Judges 13:7 Samson's mother was to be consecrated herself because of the child she carried—she was held to a Nazarite vow while carrying him. Psalm 22:10… "From my mother's womb you have been my God." Psalm 58:3 makes me realize it is a pure spirit that is not separated from God yet by sin! Jeremiah 1:5 "Before I formed you in the womb I knew you…" Spirit to spirit? Hosea 12:3 "he took his brother by the heel in the womb, and in his strength he struggled with God." Was the fighting in Rebecca's womb a spiritual battle? The spirits of these two boys fighting each other? Genesis 25—two nations? Luke 1:15 John was filled with the Holy Spirit in his mother's womb, which means he had his own spirit for God to fill. Luke 1:41, 44 John's spirit recognized the Son of God in Mary's womb while inside Elizabeth's womb! It was his spirit inside of her—not his fleshly body obviously (or his soul) that recognized the Spirit of God so close to him.

Then I wrote the following as I heard God speak it to me:

Laura, a mother who has nurtured (carried) the spirits of her children is going to be greatly entwined in her children's spiritual lives, so greatly entwined that only I can separate them—just as My Word can separate the joint and morrow, the thoughts and intents of the heart. Your children are not "who you are," but they are part of the trunk of the tree, which is greater than the branches. They spring from the very roots, and for many it takes Me to separate the two! You are okay. Part of your trunk has been chopped out and there is a bleeding that is taking place, with the healing in process. A sealing of that wound. It will be forever scarred, and sometimes may leak sap, but it will heal and is still a strong tree! (With many fruitful, flourishing branches.) This wound in the tree causes it to pull from the roots to a new depth, never before known to that tree. Any time a child goes through trauma, the mother is greatly affected. You have been chopped many, many times. This last time was a blow to previous choppings, which is why it has been so traumatic and the healing will take longer. But the character and the shade you will provide by digging in so deeply to be rooted and grounded in My love will be like no other, and beautiful to more than you will ever know in this lifetime. Yes, some will not understand or see the beauty, but I do—I created you,

knowing what every blow would become in you. I see
nothing but beauty as You allow me to do My work. Yes,
My child, there is deep healing for deep wounds. Continue
to rest in Me through this process.

So You are telling me that I can't just
receive this revelation and be on a new level,
soaring past the pain because it is a process I must
go through to be able to connect with others when
they go through a process of pain and grief? I
don't like it, don't want it, but I will accept it,
because I know You *are* love, and it must be in
Your love for me that You are doing it this way. I
wanted to have the pain be lifted… But I will be
thankful for the revelation. I know it will be used
greatly in the process of my healing. Thank You.
I want to live my life by the roots that cannot be
seen instead of the tree that can be. The roots are
who I really am. They are what I come from and
am connected to, to make the tree what it is.

Wow! Every time I read this, I am amazed
at how powerful it is. Thank You, Father God,
for Your love that never ends, and for the way
You are so very willing to comfort us and give us
wisdom and new revelation!

One day in my deep grief, I pulled out pictures of Becca.
All through that last year and a half when she had been in and
out of the hospital, we took lots and lots of pictures. She wanted
pictures taken all the time. She even wanted pictures taken of her

when she came out of her surgeries, so she could look at them later. So when it came time for her funeral, as morbid as it might sound, her husband and I both agreed we needed pictures. It just felt like something we needed to do to help complete things.

I know some of you parents will totally understand, and some of you will be appalled. My husband hates seeing those pictures of Becca's funeral (especially the ones of her lying in her casket) and will have nothing to do with them. But once in a while I actually pull them up on my computer and look at them. During one of those times, God used it as a way for me to make a conscious decision to step over an invisible line, no longer allowing myself to live in this wrong identity. Here is what I wrote at that time:

> That shaft of light on the casket is amazing! I can't believe I never noticed it in the picture before, until today.

> This is so hard! Unbelievably hard! I know there will be a shift and a change in my life when I turn off this picture...but I don't want to lose her—sounds weird, I know. It is a letting go of my identity as Becca's mom. I know there has to be a death for true life to come forth. "Unless a grain of wheat falls to the ground and dies…" (John 12:24) I asked earlier for a seed of hope to be planted in my heart. You said the seed was already there but needed to grow. Faith is the smallest seed that grows until it is big enough to provide shade and a place for the birds. I know I have to do this, and it is more than just a symbol,

but a change. I want the change, the shift. I *need* it, but it is VERY painful to say this final goodbye. And I know I need to do it soon before it gets even worse. Help me, Holy Spirit! I need Your strength. When I am weak, You are strong!

As you can see, none of this has been possible without God's help. Please allow me one last journal entry for this chapter.

1/28/12: Lord, I come here feeling so lost. I feel like I just want to be me and don't know who that is anymore! I know who You are, and I just hide myself in You.

Laura, I have called you by name! You are Mine (Isaiah 43:1).

The loss of our child shakes us to the very core of our being. The grief is more than intense; a part of us has died with our child. But it is not a place we have to camp out and stay for life. Our grief is an experience we can go through and come out on the other side, releasing ourselves with God's help from allowing it to be our identity. I am so very thankful it no longer defines who I am, and I pray you desire to have the same freedom.

The last picture we had of the two of us taken together, less than two weeks before Becca died

CHAPTER 11

||||||||||||||

The Pillars of Thoughts and Words

Your beliefs drive your thoughts. Your thoughts drive your emotions. Your emotions drive your actions. This is something I heard recently, and the more I think about it, the more I realize how true that statement is.

Our actions are based on our emotions. The way we are acting (or reacting) to the death of our child is based on our emotions. Our emotions run very deep. There is so much pain. There is so much confusion. There is darkness and a feeling of hopelessness. That is normal and natural.

But I believe with everything in me that that is not where we have to stay.

My emotions are driven by my thoughts. I can think things like *I will never get past this* or *I will always feel this way*. I know some parents even have the thought *I don't want to get past this*, which is usually because they equate the pain of grieving their child with remembering their child. They are afraid if they quit hurting so much, they will forget their child.

This is a perfect example of how your beliefs drive your thoughts. If you believe that staying in your pain will keep the memory of your child alive, then you will continue in that emotional state of despair and not be able to live a life of peace, hope, and fullness that includes walking out your God-ordained destiny.

Grounding Your Beliefs

May I make a suggestion? How about if we back this train up? Let's go to the engine of this train that is driving us: our beliefs. Not a single one of us who is experiencing life again after the death of our child has forgotten our child, in the least bit. It is very possible—in fact it is even *better*—to hold onto the memory of my child without the intense pain of those first few weeks, months, and even years.

Do you have even a glimmer of hope that it is possible? If thousands of parents have walked this path ahead of you and picked up the shattered pieces of their lives—still missing their child, but also still a part of the lives of the people who are here—can you open yourself up to that possibility?

I can visualize some of you with tears running, thinking about the turmoil this creates inside of you. A battle is going on inside your soul. You desperately want to believe this, and yet you desperately want to hold onto the only thing left of your child—your memory of them. Is it even right for you to go on with life without them? Let me release you from that thought right now. Yes, it is okay.

When my kids were younger, if they saw me sick or worried, maybe even crying, they would come up to me in their sweetness and innocence and try to make me feel better. They did not like to see their mommy hurt in any way. I know we would much rather it had been us who left this earth, but it wasn't. Do you want to honor your child by allowing your grief to cause your own death? Not living, just existing in the shell of your body? Or would you rather honor your child by living a life they could point at proudly and say, "That's my mom! That's my dad!"

I'm trying to get you to believe that maybe, just maybe, it is possible to get past this—to think *others have, and maybe I can too.*

I remember exactly when I grabbed hold of that belief; it was a turning point for me. I was standing in the cemetery, crying at Becca's grave. I stood there and looked around at all those other tombstones. I knew many of them were for children or young adults because I had spent many hours walking around reading the tombstones, including the dates, and figuring out how old they were when they were buried. I thought about how every single one of those tombstones had a story of the people who were left behind, who had grieved and mourned. Every one of those tombstones represented someone's pain and loss.

It suddenly hit me that all of these people (including those who had buried a child) somehow managed to get through it. And somehow I could too. That realization planted a tiny seed of hope that I didn't have to stay in this dark place, which gave me what I needed to slowly start working my way out of the black pit.

Believing the truth is just as powerful as believing a lie.

People do what they do, based on their feelings, because of what they believe. Most people live mainly out of their feelings, and feelings do not always equal the truth. To put that a different way, just because I have feelings about something, no matter how strong, does not mean my feelings are necessarily based on the truth.

To change your behavior, which is driven by your emotions, you must know and understand the truth. It is truth that will set you free. To experience victory in any area of your life, you must overcome limiting beliefs in that area.

I don't remember exactly what it was, but many years ago I was asking God to change or fix something in my life. He asked me which prayer I wanted answered. I wasn't sure what He meant. He reminded me of my consistent prayer for Him to do whatever He needed to get me where He wanted me to be. He then let me know that whatever this was I was praying against was something He wanted to use to get me where He wanted me to be.

So at that point I needed to make a decision. Did I want God to answer this immediate prayer and take me out of my misery, or did I want Him to answer the other prayer by allowing the situation to do a work in my life—getting me to where He wanted me to be? As I said, I don't remember what that situation was, but I do remember I took the "fix it" prayer off the table and stayed with my prayer of "do whatever You want to get me where You want me to be."

Over the years I've been faced with that same decision over and over again. This subject reminds me of something I recently wrote for my Kidz Korner blog. What determines God's goodness? Is He good because He answers my prayers the way I want Him to? Is that what makes a person good? Because they give us what we want to make us happy? Or are they good because they know how to make right decisions for everyone involved? Are they good because they are not willing to compromise in the moment, but hold fast because they see and know the greater good further down the road?

I find it very sad when people walk away from God because He didn't give them the answer they wanted to a prayer. God is not a vending machine where we put in the prayer, push a button, and the solution we want drops out for us.

We have a two-year-old granddaughter. She is being taught to say please and is learning that just because she says "pleeeeease" doesn't mean she automatically gets what she wants.

When you ask someone for something, they have a choice to say yes or no. When we ask God for something, He has the choice to say yes or no. Did I want Him to say yes and allow Becca to stay here on this earth? Of course I did, with every fiber of my being! As a matter of fact, I believed He was actually going to heal her heart, either through a miracle or through a heart transplant. As I stated earlier, I was totally blindsided when she died—even though she was very sick. Once again I was forced to face that bottom-line prayer I have prayed almost all my life, of giving God permission to do whatever He wanted to do to get me where He wanted me to be. And this time it cost me an *extremely* high price.

Do I believe God killed my daughter to use it in some way in my life? ABSOLUTELY NOT! Do I believe that God allowed the natural consequences of a fallen and sinful world to take effect, not stopping it, even though many people were praying for her healing? Yes, I do. Do I still give Him permission to do what He wants to do as God, instead of what I want Him to do, because He can see so much more than I can see? ABSOLUTELY!

I have chosen not to change my thoughts and beliefs on who God is just because I did not get a prayer answered the way I wanted Him to, no matter how painful it may be.

To get through this to be able to live again, we cannot lean on our own understanding. In all our ways we have to acknowledge the truth that God is always good, whether we agree with His decisions or not. In order to change my feelings, I have to change my perspective.

The Bible tells us Jonah was thrown into the sea by the ship's crew to stop a violent storm. Then the Lord sent a great fish to swallow the rebellious prophet, and we can read his prayer from inside that fish. "I have been expelled from your sight. Nevertheless, I will look again toward your holy temple" Jonah 2:4 (NASB). Even in what looked like a totally hopeless situation, Jonah had hope. "While I was fainting away, I remembered the Lord, and my prayer came to you in your holy Temple....Salvation is from the Lord" Jonah 2:7,9 (NASB). The Lord is always ready to offer us salvation, which is an ongoing complete deliverance.

Too often we sit back in our pain and grief and wait for some sort of miracle to happen in front of us when the miracle is already inside us. The miraculous isn't something we strive for; it is something we were created for. When Peter wanted to walk on water, Jesus didn't reprimand him for saying, "IF you are Jesus...." He just said, "Come!"

I wrote the following journal entries in faith of what I was declaring to be true, six weeks after Becca's death (along with a response from my Daddy God):

11/29/11: Psalm 91:9 "You have made the Lord, who is my refuge, even the Most High, your dwelling place" Lord, I want that! Teach me how to make You my dwelling place. Psalm 71:3 "Be to me a rock of habitation to which I may continually come" (NASB). I want You to be my rock of habitation!

11/30/11: I need a renewed mind. I need to change my thoughts, the way I think. My mind is a key to be renewed, which will enable me to come into that place of rest. It has been so obvious to me the last few days that my thoughts are heavy, which makes my soul and countenance heavy. I need a breakthrough; it is in my thoughts. God, I give You permission to renew my mind or show me how to do it if I need to do it myself. Refresh my thoughts so that my soul and very being will be refreshed. Someone told me that knowing who I am as a daughter is enough, a matter of life or death for me. Is that true, God? Is it that critical for me?

Yes, My daughter, for you have been beaten down since you were a child. Your spirit is very close to the breaking point of not ever being or doing enough and shutting yourself off from everyone, and that would eventually include Me. I refuse to allow you to be a war casualty. When a soldier is wounded in battle, he comes to a place of rest and healing. You have been wounded over and over and have never allowed yourself to be in My hospital of rest and healing long enough for a full recovery. It is time! It is time, before the effects of the wounds of the battles become more than you can overcome.

When God created us, He did an amazing thing. One of the ways He made us in His image is by allowing us to think our own thoughts. He does not control our thoughts, even though He could. He allows us to think He is the evil one. I remember times when my kids blamed me for something and were angry at me when I wasn't the one who caused the pain, or my decision was based on something I could see that they could not. It's the same way with God. He allows us to have our own thoughts, even if we believe a lie about Him. That is how much He loves us. He doesn't force us to trust Him or love Him. He lets it come from our own choice and our own thoughts.

The only powers great enough to keep me from living out my kingdom inheritance here on earth are lies and deception. We are secure in God and His blood covenant through Jesus. Even if we falter through life, He will never let go of our hand. That makes it sound like it's easy, but it still requires a deep level of trust, based on believing that His love and wisdom will take us through the best way. Don't let the enemy take the greatest pain and darkness you have ever faced and turn it into a lie that God doesn't love you, or that He has turned His back on you.

The only way to get out of the enemy's sticky web is to still your soul, quiet your own thoughts, and ask God to give you His thoughts. You need to be transformed—totally changed—by the renewing of your mind (Romans 12:2). Allow God's thoughts to speak softly to you in the depths of your being to set you free from the turmoil. Sit quietly in His presence, letting His thoughts reprogram your thinking.

What you focus on is what you will grow. So if you continue to focus on the pain and loss, it will grow until it is ready to consume you and overtake you. But if instead you think about, focus on, and give thanks for what or who you still have, that is what will begin to grow, and eventually it will bring you out of that deep dark place. And you may not think so right now, but you can actually get to the place where you celebrate your child's life, instead of being stuck in the pain of their death.

I remember reading somewhere that the only way out of the anger is through gratitude. When we make the choice to flip the switch and find things to be thankful for, we will start to see a change happening in our lives and feel the pain of loss lighten.

The Bible tells us that we are to take every thought captive to make it obedient to Christ (2 Corinthians 10:5). Our thoughts become our words. Words are powerful. We see that all through Scripture. For something to be released we have to decree it, we have to declare it. We don't have to feel it, but somehow we have to push through to get ourselves to speak the truth of what God says. We can't just wish this pain wouldn't be so intense. We need to speak God into the circumstance, into our pain.

I heard God speak to me about the way I was thinking, well over a year after I lost Becca, as seen in the journal entry below.

> 1/16/13: *Let's go back to perspective. You have been stuck on how difficult your life has been. I want you to spend some time meditating on the good, on the blessings, on the wonderful and joyful things. Let's "reprogram" you and your thought process!*

Reprogramming Your Thoughts

One of the thoughts that had to be reprogrammed was how I didn't want to be two years or five years or ten years further away from Becca! That thought could become overwhelming, causing such a panic that I almost couldn't breathe!

I asked God to help me by giving me His thoughts. I found myself realizing the truth is actually something totally different from what was in my thoughts. Every day I live on this earth brings me closer to my own departure date, and closer to Becca, not further away from her! Wow! The truth set me free! I still have moments when I have those thoughts, and they can still make me cry. But I am not overwhelmed by them, as I now believe a truth that is deeper than my pain: I am getting closer to her, not further away from her.

Something else that helped me was to realize God isn't just "out there" somewhere. He is actually inside me. Because I have invited Jesus to be Lord of my life, the Spirit of God dwells in me. I don't have to wait for God to come to me from somewhere out there. I can quiet myself and listen to His still small voice from inside of me, speaking peace, bringing comfort. Whatever I need, He is already inside of me to meet that need. The amazing thing is that He is also sitting on His throne at the exact same time. And I can come boldly to that throne of our gracious God to receive His mercy and find His help which I so desperately need (Hebrews 4:16).

For over three years after Becca died, it really bothered me I could not find the notes I read at her funeral. Writing this book has caused me to dig in all kinds of places to find what I wanted to share, and I finally found that piece of paper. I can't tell you how surreal it was to finally have it in front of me.

The name Rebecca means faithful. And she has now heard the words "Well done, good and faithful servant. Enter into the joy of your

Lord!" She knew it was time to hear those words and she was ready.

It is all a matter of perspective.

Romans 8:18-25, "Yet what we suffer now is nothing compared to the glory He will reveal to us later. For all creation is waiting eagerly for that future day when God will reveal who his children really are. Against its will, all creation was subjected to God's curse. But with eager hope, the creation looks forward to the day when it will join God's children in glorious freedom from death and decay. For we know that all creation has been groaning as in the pains of childbirth right up to the present time. And we believers also groan, even though we have the Holy Spirit within us as a foretaste of future glory, for we long for our bodies to be released from sin and suffering. We, too, wait with eager hope for the day when God will give us our full rights as his adopted children, including the new bodies he has promised us. We were given this hope when we were saved. (If we already have something, we don't need to hope for it. But if we look forward to something we don't yet have, we must wait patiently and confidently.)" (NLT)

Second Corinthians 4:8-9 is actually the verse to a song she used to sing on the worship team at church, always singing it as a solo—her personal declaration in the midst of what she was dealing with. "We are hard pressed on every side, but not crushed; perplexed, but not in despair;

persecuted, but not abandoned; struck down, but not destroyed" (NIV). The song goes on to say how we are blessed beyond the curse because His promises will endure; that His joy is going to be my strength. It talks about trading our sorrows, our sickness, and our pain for the joy of the Lord.

The chapter goes on in verses 17-18 and on into the next chapter, "For our light and momentary troubles are achieving for us an eternal glory that far outweighs them all. So we fix our eyes not on what is seen, but on what is unseen, since what is seen is temporary, but what is unseen is eternal. For we know that if the earthly tent we live in is destroyed, we have a building from God, an eternal house in heaven, not built by human hands. So we groan, longing to be clothed instead with our heavenly dwelling…so that what is mortal may be swallowed up by life" (NIV).

Becca is actually now more alive than we are!

I believed every word of that when I spoke it. I believed every word of that in the blackness of depression. And I still believe it with every fiber of my being today.

CHAPTER 12

|||||||||||||||

The Cornerstone of Trust

At this point, we have looked at the blueprints for rebuilding most of our house, but we have left out something very important. The cornerstone is crucial because it determines how everything else fits into place.

There are only two things that will cause you to trust someone. You either trust someone because you are in a relationship with them and know them personally, or because someone you personally trust convinces you to trust that third person. In other words, because you trust someone, you can trust who they trust.

I hope at this point I fall into that second category. As a parent who has lost a child, I have gone through the trauma, grief, and darkness that come with it. I am also someone who was able to plant a seed of hope in my life that is now growing into a tree of life. It is a different tree with different fruit from before Becca died, but it is alive and sprouting and starting to bear some fruit. You are still reading, which means something I am saying is drawing you to believe there is hope for you too, and that you trust me to give you some tools to help get you to that place.

So as someone you are learning to trust, I want to tell you who I trust. In case you haven't been able to tell, I fully trust God, even after all of Becca's sicknesses He could have healed but did not, and yes, even after He didn't stop her death but allowed her to go to her eternal home ahead of me. And I fully believe you can and need to trust God as well.

I don't really believe there is a way I can "teach" you how to trust God. I think the best way is to show you how others and I have done it.

As you have seen throughout this book, journaling has been an important piece of my healing. As I write whatever it is I need to say, often a new piece of healing revelation will come. Many other grieving parents have discovered the same thing.

Let me back up right now to my first journal entry after Becca passed. It was three days later, two days before her funeral.

10/15/11: Where do I even start? Becca, I love you! I miss you. This is very hard, but it is good for you. You are now living Romans 8:18! ("I consider that our present sufferings are not worth comparing with the glory that will be revealed in us" NIV.)

God, so many things You have shown me, and yet still there are so many things I don't understand.

Thank You for Your love. Thank You for the strength You are giving me through the prayers of others. Thank You for the life of Becca, thank You for her release in You. Thank You, Daddy, for letting me just be with You this morning! Pour into me what needs to be poured in, for You know...You know what I need more than I know myself.

Thank You, Father, for the new richness I am finding in Your Word concerning death—Becca's death. Romans 8, 2 Corinthians 4 and 5, Ephesians 3. I am reading these things with new eyes, such as mortality is swallowed up by life (2 Corinthians 5:4)...wow!

Becca is in the real world now! She is living the reality of eternity with Father God in Jesus!

Here is my next entry, six days later:

10/21/11: Jesus, I feel so lost right now—what is this? What do You want from me? How do I go deeper? How do I get more of You? Why do I feel so empty and dissatisfied right now? I feel so broken! Why am I not seeing You? Why am I not feeling You? Where are You?

Laura, will you quit coming to Me?

Of course not!

Why not?

Because I am going to pursue You no matter what!

Why?

Because I need You. Because You are worth pursuing. Because I know only You have what I need.

> *…You may not have seen, heard, or felt anything, but you are faithful! That, My dear, is a big thing. When you are faithful in the little, I can give much. Go in peace and know that you have done well.*

This was such a comfort to me, that God would let me know it was okay to be so confused, hurt, lost, and broken. I look back at it now and wonder how I couldn't see that this turmoil should have been expected, based on how fresh my grief was. But at least I knew I needed Him to get me through it.

Stay on the Operating Table

One day I was telling God how badly I wanted to be done with the pain. I wanted to be healed from what was being done to me. I heard God tell me to "stay on the operating table." Here is my response to that word from Him.

12/13/11: You are using all of this to answer my prayers to purify me! I humble myself and submit to the work You are doing. It is the answer to my prayers of Ezekiel 47—the river— to be at the place where I can no longer stand and be in control. You have brought me to this place, and I choose to go for it! This is the river from Your throne that brings LIFE! And within that comes the place of rest in Hebrews 3 and 4. It wasn't unbelief in God. They believed in God, but they failed to believe that He is good! That place of rest comes from believing He is good. I know He is good, but I couldn't see what was happening, why I was struggling so much with all these feelings. Forgive me, Lord, for doubting— nothing can touch me unless You allow it. You are pulling up the dross and skimming it off to purify me. And You LOVE me! You are with me through this ugliness and You still love me deeply! You are also answering the prayer I have had for the last several years of Ephesians 3:16- 19 to truly know Your love and be so immersed in the knowledge of Your love for me that it flows naturally from me to those around me. I had no idea how deeply You are at work in me, and even though it is very painful, it is marvelous and will be worth it!

This actually brought me to a new level of freedom in my journey. God was not the cause of my pain, but He was using the painful journey to do a work in me. It is not going to be wasted in my life!

What I was discovering is that for many years I cried out to God to make me dead to myself and alive to Him and Him only. I don't want to walk in my own flesh on this earth. And so, because I gave Him permission to do whatever it takes to get me where He wants me to be, He took me up on that and allowed the worst possible thing to happen in my life, the death of one of my children. That caused me to die in so many ways, as you have also experienced. And then He began to use that event to rebuild me as an answer to my own prayers.

I am not saying that anyone who prays "Lord, do what You want to do with me" is going to have a child die. And I am definitely not saying God killed my daughter! What I am saying is that He allowed it to happen, knowing how He would use it in my life and in the lives of my husband, our children, and other people who were greatly affected by her death. If I am truly honest, I know I am still working toward fully believing that this is a win-win situation for all of us. I am walking in a deeper level with God than I knew existed before, and my daughter, who was so ill and struggling on this earth, is now whole and dancing in heaven with Jesus. While it is so very wrong to have to bury your own child, and it took me to an extremely dark and painful place, I know she is through facing the pain, the tears, and the trials of this world.

When I dwell on my pain and my loss of not having Becca here with me for however long I am here on this earth, the tears can still run freely. But when I focus on where she is and how free she is, the pain begins to lessen.

Becca is sitting in her wheelchair in the exact spot at the University of Wisconsin Hospital where she prayed to receive Jesus during one of her cancer treatments at four years old (only then she was sitting in a little red wagon).

As you can see, there are times I still struggle. I still go back and forth in my emotions and the level of pain I feel from not having Becca here to share my life, as shown below.

> 6\7\12: I sit here now with such a mixture of emotions I do not understand. I feel like I could use a good cry and am fighting the tears, and yet I'm also in a place of peace and contentment sitting here on the porch swing. How can that be?

Laura, it is a division of your soul and spirit.
Your spirit is at rest, but your soul is hurting.

So what do I do with it?

Nothing right now. Just know that I love you and
that ALL of My words are true. Just keep waiting for
My loving kindness. It is all around you, and it will begin
advancing toward you. Yes, I will beautify the afflicted
ones with salvation (Psalm 149:4). *You will be saved*
from the enemy, from his attacks, from others who are
doing you wrong, and it will be beautiful—you will be
beautiful—because you will be an even greater reflection
of My Son and His love!

Sometimes we think we can't trust unless we know the
"why." Since I am a child of God, I often use my own experience
as a parent to help me understand my heavenly Father. Are there
times I need my children to trust me without giving them an
explanation? Of course. Are there lots of reasons I might not
tell them why? Yes. And I know there are times my children have
asked why (or why not), not because they really want to know,
but because they want to be able to argue against my reason,
whatever that reason is.

We can have the same attitude with God. Even if He told
us why, it wouldn't be a good enough reason for the moment in
our intense pain and darkness, and we just want to argue with
Him on how wrong He was to do this to us.

Understanding will never bring us peace. That is why
we are told to trust in God and not in our own understanding
(Proverbs 3:5). For some reason we often think if *we* can figure

things out *we* can be in control. But the relief felt doesn't last very long. Soon there is something else we are trying to make sense of. I have heard it said the problem is we are searching for mastery instead of seeking the Master Himself.

> 6/21/12: God, my faith has been shaken and is weak right now. Bring me to the words in Your Scriptures that will grow my faith. I need You to help me, Holy Spirit, to increase my faith for the breakthrough I need!

> ...Thank You, God! You have shown me it is okay that Becca passed on and received her healing on the other side, because I kept my faith to the end. I was blindsided *because* of my faith, and that pleased You....thank You, God, for showing me this. You just answered my cry to restore my faith. You are so good!

This is something I never would have known if I had insisted on my own understanding and not looked to God for His. Is it any wonder I love Him so much and trust Him? And yet I know there is room to trust Him so much more than I do.

> 1/28/13: Holy Spirit, help me to remember that the events in Joseph's life were to position him in his place of destiny. You used the horrible circumstances in his life to put him exactly where he needed to be. Help me to trust You more fully! I believe, help my unbelief.

In this place of learning to trust God with our lives, no matter what He allows to happen to us, we will all move at a different pace. We have different levels of what we have to offer God. Sometimes we can offer Him "everything," other times just one tiny crumb. That's okay. And sometimes it takes everything we have to trust Him. That's okay too.

Every step on our life journey is actually a step of trust. We either trust in others, in ourselves, or in God. What happens when it is more than a step and we need to take a giant leap of chasms in the dark? What about when we have to scale steep mountains, not knowing what is at the top? And then there is this valley of death we are crossing through. These are the times when trusting completely in others or ourselves will eventually fail. Only God knows the difficulty we face, and where the best place is to step, for each part of our life journey. The best thing we can do is take our eyes off the journey and focus on the One who never leaves our side as He helps us through the next step on the path.

I know a woman who has been fighting cancer for more than two years in a knock-down drag-out fight—her second round of it. Some days she feels well, but those times are sandwiched between days on end of pain and suffering. More and more often she doesn't have the strength to type her short daily blog, and it goes unwritten until she has the strength or someone else steps in and tells us her circumstances, asking for prayer. She now has twenty-four-hour hospice care. Even in all her trials, she trusts God and what He is allowing in her life, drawing close to Him in a way not known to many here on this earth. She wrote the following:

Adversity brings out the worst or the best in people....When you are met with adversity, what is your perspective? Do you open up communication with God or shut yourself away to complain? Consider opening yourself to your faith and trusting in the Lord's plan instead of questioning it.

Lori Burns – CaringBridge blog 10/10/14

Note: While writing this book, Lori passed on to meet her Lord face-to-face.

Faith = Trust

Life is hard but God is still good. He told us we would face hard things in our lives here on earth. There is suffering in this world because of the curse of sin. God created a perfect world. He put man in that world He created. Man chose to rebel and disobey God, which brought a curse on all mankind. This world is now broken and doesn't work the way God created it to work. He had a plan for how to bring us back to a place of being right with Him, and that was through His Son Jesus Christ being sent here as a man to live on earth. He paid a high price to make things right. He gave His life. And that's where we are right now, because there's more to the story yet to come. We won't be made completely new until we cross over into eternity, but it will happen if we put our trust and belief in Jesus and the price He paid for us.

Trust and faith are pretty much the same thing. In fact, I have a Bible that was translated by a Messianic Jewish scholar

(*The Complete Jewish Bible* by David H. Stern), and he doesn't use "Christianese" but rather words that are a more literal translation as a Jew. The word *faith* isn't used. He always uses the word *trust*, and it really opened my eyes to help me realize that faith isn't something I have to figure out how to do or have enough of. It is simply choosing to trust in God.

Hebrews 11 is a great example of this. Verse 1 reads, "Trusting is being confident of what we hope for, convinced about things we do not see." The entire chapter talks about how "by trusting," each person did what they did for God. Sometimes I struggle to figure out how to get more faith. Yes, I know faith comes by hearing the Word of God and so on, but sometimes faith just seems so far away to get to. But trust? I can do that.

Romans 1:17 in this translation reads, "... but the person who is righteous will live his life by trust." It is amazing how changing that one word somehow seems to make it easier for me. Faith just seems so abstract and something I have to try to reach for. But trust is something I can easily choose to rest in.

I can choose to believe there is no God or He would have saved my child. I can choose to believe that if there is a God, He isn't good and He isn't fair or He would have saved my child. Both of those options leave me feeling angry and empty. I have chosen the third option. There is a God, His thoughts and ways are so much higher than mine, He loves me with a perfect love, and even though I don't understand why He has allowed this to happen, I still trust Him with my life both here on earth and for eternity. This option has brought me to a place of peace, rest, hope, and life again—even within the pain.

Death is a part of life. We will all die at some point. And as painful as it is, some of us will have children who leave this earth ahead of us. The question is how are we going to choose to live the rest of our lives when they are gone and there is nothing we can do to bring them back?

During grief, people either move toward God or away from Him. But when we move away from Him, we are moving away from the One who can help us the most. God wants to walk with us through this valley of death. He wants to give us comfort. He wants to give us strength. He wants to give us hope. These are all things we desperately need. But if we choose to move away from Him, we will continue to desperately need these things. This is a time to get as close to God as you possibly can.

As I was writing the last paragraph, I got a picture of a distraught child crying uncontrollably. In the picture, I see a father bending down to pick up that child. The child is so upset he is kicking and screaming and fighting the father, who is trying to pick him up. Eventually the child runs out of strength and relaxes in the embrace of his loving father. And now that child can receive the comfort, strength, and hope he wants and needs. It is the same with us. Don't fight the One who can give you the very things you need. Surrender, let Him embrace you and carry you in His strong arms of love.

Choose to trust His love for you, even when you can't see it or feel it.

Here is something I recently heard from God.

Laura, My daughter, I have a love for you that is so special and so deep and so unique that I can't love anyone else with it. It is a love that is only for you! No one else can receive it because it is yours and yours only!

I would like you to receive this word for yourself right now. Put your own name in it because this isn't just a message for me.

> **_____, I have a love for you that is so special and so deep and so unique that I can't love anyone else with it. It is a love that is only for you! No one else can receive it because it is yours and yours only!**

How about if you make it even more personal? Try it again. Read this out loud to yourself. (Remember, your words have power.)

> **God has a love for *me* that is so special and so deep and so unique that He can't love anyone else with it. It is a love that is only for me! No one else can receive it because it is mine and mine only!**

Say it again if you need to. Keep saying it until the truth of it breaks through and you know in your heart that because of His incredible, extravagant love for you, you can trust Him.

Once you have made a decision to trust God, you can get specific about the areas where you need His help. From that place of trust, begin to talk to Him and tell Him exactly what you need in your place of grief and pain. He wants to hear from you, and He wants to help you through this dark place. Hebrews 4:16 (NLT) says, "So let us come boldly to the throne of our gracious God. There we will receive His mercy, and we will find grace to help us when we need it most."

I like to read through a different version of the Bible every year. I underline, I highlight, and I write notes to myself right on the pages when God speaks something to me about what I just read. I would like to end this chapter by sharing one of these notes with you.

First Peter 5:6-7 says, "Therefore, humble yourselves under the mighty hand of God, that He may exalt you at the proper time, casting all your anxiety on Him, because He cares for you" (NASB). Next to that verse I wrote, "I cast everything on the Lord and trust Him to take care of it ALL."

If you still can't seem to agree with that in your own heart right now, I pray that you will very soon.

CHAPTER 13

||||||||||||||||||

Putting on the Roof of Hope

After Becca's death, I had no one I knew of who had lost a child that I could cry with, no one who would understand my pain and tell me I wasn't going crazy! And so many of the books I read didn't give much hope of ever coming out of the place of darkness I found myself in. I knew that in Christ there is *always* hope and life and destiny and good things. My life didn't end when my daughter's did, even though it felt like it with every fiber of my being. It was like my soul died, but my spirit didn't.

The battle was on. Would I remain with a dead soul, living the rest of my life out of an empty shell, or would I allow the life of the Spirit inside to resurrect me and breathe new life into my soul so I could actually *live* out my days on earth in fullness?

This chapter is for anyone struggling to have hope, especially if you feel there is no hope for you to even feel hope! To be able to write this chapter, I had to come from that place of hopelessness myself.

Once again, I want to share with you from my journal how God brought me along the way, teaching me to hope in the midst of darkness.

11/24/11: Daddy, can I please see my Becca sometime? Please? I want to see her whole—I want to see her in glory. I want to see her full of Your joy. I want to see her, please? What has she been doing? Is it okay for me to ask this of You?

My dear daughter, yes, it is okay for you to ask, of course. But that doesn't mean I will answer. There is a moment while on earth that I will pull back heaven and you will see her. You need to be content with that. It will happen sometime.

12/5/11: I am out on the balcony reading *Hinds' Feet on High Places.* She found that flower named Joy of Acceptance (after seeing the places where the grain was being crushed, the clay was being molded, and the gold was being heated). I began meditating on that—joy with acceptance. The tears came when I asked, "Why me? Why was I chosen to bear such heavy things?" But the real pain came when the question was, "Am I done or is there more?" (An hour and a half later I returned to my journal.) I played the Misty Edwards song "Fling Wide." Wow! Talk about touching me where I was! I was able to open my heart to God, not even realizing I had begun to shut Him off because of my pain. Thank You, Daddy, for Your open arms! ...I started to realize how much He loves me, to send me on this cruise. That's pretty extravagant love! I think maybe I can become that flower of the joy of acceptance...

12/29/11: I see myself crossing a log above a huge chasm, but as long as I look at Jesus and hold His hand while crossing, I will make it! I will keep stepping! I will keep walking. I will look to You, not to the log or the chasm that I'm crossing, but just at You, Jesus.

1/20/12: So much of life is based on our perspective! More than I ever realized.

Yes, My child, I want to give you new eyes, a new heart, and a new mind. For you become what you look and gaze upon. Gaze upon Me—on My beauty, on My love for you—and it will change your perspective!

He led me to Philippians 4:4-8. Verse 8 says, "Finally, brethren, whatever things are true, whatever things are noble, whatever things are just, whatever things are pure, whatever things are lovely, whatever things are of good report, if there is any virtue and if there is anything praiseworthy—meditate on these things."

I actually wrote down each portion of this verse and then made myself think of those things and write them down, such as "whatever things are true." I wrote a whole page of what was true in my life, truth based on what God says. And I went through the whole verse that way. I highly suggest you do the same thing for yourself.

> [Journal entry, no date]: Romans 15:13 "Now may the God of hope fill you with all joy and peace in believing, that you may abound in hope by the power of the Holy Spirit." Joy, peace, and hope is a "filling" by You. I come into agreement with what Paul asked; I pray the God of hope will fill me with all joy and peace in believing, so that I will abound in hope by the power of the Holy Spirit. I speak God's hope into my hopelessness! And from that hope come joy and peace.
>
> 3/9/12: Thank You, Holy Spirit. I had gotten to the point where I didn't want a long life anymore! But You gave me a reason to want to stick around—to be there for my grandchildren and great-grandchildren. To be the love and rock and wisdom and guidance they will need. I want to be here for my grandchildren! With that new hope and revelation, I can once again claim verses like Psalm 91:16: "With long life I will satisfy him."
>
> 3/11/12: Nothing is too difficult, nothing is impossible for You. So if You are in me, then nothing is too difficult or impossible for me.
>
> 3/16/12: Why do I feel so blah? Yesterday afternoon I cried a lot. It was rough. I feel defeated, I feel lost, I feel weak. When does

Your strength come into my weakness? I am trying to breathe You in and breathe out the stress, the bad, whatever is not Yours. How and when do I rise above my feelings and start living in faith? When do I get to have Your joy unspeakable and full of glory? Am I supposed to just rest in You? Am I supposed to fight through this? Everyone else is in war and battles, and here I sit...I'm not helping to build the wall. I'm just here. I feel so wounded and helpless and I don't like it at all! What am I missing? I am not an example to follow. I am a benefit to no one—I'm just here. I don't want to give in (or continue giving in) to this helpless and lost feeling, but I don't know how to get out...this is crazy, it is stupid. I feel exactly like the sheltie and lost lamb picture—someone call for help for me!

I grew up with this picture in our house. It was given to Becca (since she loved Shelties) and now I have it hanging above my office desk.

Laura…I want you hidden deeply in Me right now. Stay here a while longer…trust me—trust what I am doing in you.

Lord, I feel so weak and useless, so defeated.

That's okay, My child. You are going to learn to call on Me and depend on Me totally and completely. I need you in this place now so I can place you strategically where I want you later. Can you hold on in this place? I AM here with you!

Lord, whittle away. I will wait while You do this carved work, whatever it is…just be my strength and my hope through it, please!

3/17/12: I have been thinking about how I am in the process of healing from a heart transplant….When I think of what I know of Becca's 3 surgeries, I can see the parallels. I am recovering from heart surgery, and it's okay to have the all-over emotions that I do right now. It will get better as I heal! Thank You, Holy Spirit.

And I just want to write how yesterday when I asked You on a scale of one to ten where I am with You, and You said a ten, that gave me some hope! You told me I am right where You want me to be. I was just chilling and hanging out with You, and I was okay with it—to just do nothing but "be" even if that "being" was in weariness and heaviness. Thank You again, Holy Spirit.

3/19/12: So God, what exactly is underneath all the layers You keep peeling off?

A heart of gold, tried in the fire, full of My grace and mercy and compassion and righteous judgment. My heart is in your heart, and it will shine brightly! Stay in the process and keep taking the steps I am leading you in. You are doing well, My child, very well. Stay with it, allow Me to set you free, and I can and will use you to set others free—to release My heart in them!

5/20/12: God's power to restore is so much greater than the enemy's power to destroy!

4/11/12: Jeremiah 17:7-8 *Yes, My child, let's look at this together.... You are* blessed *because you trust Me, and you trust* in *Me. You are like a tree planted by the water. You have always made sure that no matter what you are going through, I am your source. Yes, you have not realized it, but Psalm 1 is one of the main themes of your life. You spent time meditating in that scripture years ago, asking Me to make this be you. Remember, whatever you pray in My name according to My will, you shall have whatever you ask for.*

It has been a process (yes, that word again) but this is you—*a tree firmly planted by the streams of water (Me). You yield fruit in your season, your leaves do not wither, and you are still going to be coming into "whatever you do prospers." You do not fear when the heat comes because you know if you put yourself in Me you will be okay. Once again your leaves are green. You have* not *withered and died because even if you had some bad roots, you have always made sure you had roots growing toward Me and My supply for you.*

Just like the eagle whose molting is a process, not all at once so he can still hunt and is never vulnerable, your change has been a process and you have always continued to have green leaves for others to see. You may have felt dead, but there has been continual life flowing through you as you have stayed connected to Me. You can't be connected to Me, the source of all life, and not have life that produces more life.

"It will not be anxious in a year of drought." We are working on that, aren't we? Do you see why you do not need to be anxious about anything?! *If your roots go to Me as your source, it doesn't matter what comes your way, from satanic attacks to misguided Christian leaders; I will keep you green and bearing fruit in your seasons.*

It is the river from My throne room....You have been asking to see yourself the way I see you. Well, daughter, this is how I see you! My love never fails!

12/14/12: Laura, don't look at where you've been, look at where you're going! It is time to move out on the path I am lighting up for you with hope, joy, and expectancy of the good things I have for you. It is time to close the door on the darkness, the deep valley, for I am now taking you up.

And just like you didn't know the darkness could be so deep and dark, you will find out you didn't know My light could be so bright!

Even in the darkness you have stayed in the path as you held so tightly to My hand when all you could see was black and darkness. You followed Me well. You didn't let go and start grasping to find your own way, but you clung to Me even tighter....You had literal blind faith in Me! My heart sorrows for you in the pain, but I could also see where I was leading you. Now you will begin to see as well.

Feel the warmth and glory of the light as you are being led out of the dark forest. Rest in Me. There will be a short season of rest by My still waters before taking you on.

God, I can see the deep dark forest with several paths leading out. I realize many people are led in there, but then they let go of You and try to find their own way out, instead of letting the Holy Spirit lead them through. They come out on a shorter, different path than where You wanted to take them through to the other side.

Laura, Psalm 94:18 has been true for you. "When I said my foot is slipping, your unfailing love, Lord, supported me." You have always cried out to me and never let go. Just keep stepping each day where I lead you. As you come out of the darkness, I need you to cling to Me as tightly as you did in the darkness!

Now I want you to read what a few other parents have to say. Consider them the shingles on the roof. These are various comments and testimonies of how they got to the place of hope (taken from several different posts on Facebook groups). I believe the more parents you hear from who found hope, the easier it is to grab hold of the rope being offered you.

<u>L.S.</u> "My twenty-two-year-old daughter was killed in a tragic car accident. Before she died in the accident, since she was very involved in church activities and a strong believer of Jesus, she asked me if I ever thought about going to church. After she died, out of respect and in honor of her suggestion, I started to attend church every week. Then I got involved in their senior high youth group. I was filled with JOY, encouragement, hugs, and surrounded by laughter and enthusiasm of between sixty and one hundred fifty teens, depending on the night, of those AWESOME teens. I developed so many great bonds over the eight years I was a sponsor that I started attending students' events that they participated in at their high schools—show choir, band and choral concerts, sports and dance and performing arts activities, invites to birthday parties, and hundreds of graduation parties and commencement invites and now weddings over the eight years I was a sponsor. The teens did not replace my daughter, but they filled my life with JOY and a purpose for living again. I still miss my daughter every day, but I try to remember if I was the one who had died, I would want her to live as normal a life as possible."

<u>D.S.</u> "When we lost our sixteen-year-old son in 2003, I wanted to just climb inside myself and never come out. I felt that NO ONE understood what I was going through. Then,

I believe it was God who gave me an inspiring thought that has gotten me through all these years. How would my SON want me to act? Would he want his passing to make me into a shell of my former self? Or would he want to know that I could honor his life by making the best of mine? Sometimes, even eleven years later, I have to ask myself, "Would this behavior please your son?" This also allowed me to be a mother again to our surviving son."

<u>J.O.</u> "After almost seven years from the loss of our son, joy can coexist with sorrow and we can respectfully live with both! We can very clearly see the one set of footprints where He carried us! We are beginning to celebrate his life with love and laughter and that's good! We have missed that! I think my healing may take a lifetime. I'm a mom, but what I know is that as I walk through this journey, I will embrace the joy and the tears, I will embrace the happy and the sad! It has taken me a while; grief is the hardest thing I have ever done, but I refused, after I heard a young girl who had lost her sister say, "The day my sister died, my mom died too; she is just still breathing!" Ouch for this mother's heart!

<u>K.C.</u> "So hard to believe it has been seventeen years today that my beautiful girl went to be with Jesus. So thankful that with Christ in

my life, I don't have to grieve as one with no hope. I will forever be thankful for the time we had."

Waiting, Trusting, Hoping

I read somewhere that waiting, trusting, and hoping are like three strands of a rope. Trust is the middle strand, and hope and waiting are the two strands that wrap around it. This is a good description of how I have gotten to the place I have, with the grace of God.

"Brothers and sisters, we do not want you to…grieve like the rest of mankind, who have no hope" (1 Thessalonians 4:13 NIV).

When I talk about hope I am not talking about wishful thinking. I am talking about something we know is coming that we anticipate. A great example is a little girl who hopes she will get married someday. That is the wishful thinking kind of hope. But one day a young man comes into her life, they fall deeply in love, and he gets down on one knee with a question and a ring. Her getting married is no longer wishful thinking. It is something she actually starts planning for with anticipation, knowing it is coming.

That is the kind of hope God talks about and gives us in the Bible. Wishful thinking won't get you out of your black hole of grief, but hope will. True hope. The anticipation of knowing that God will pull you out and put you on a path of life that leads you to fullness and satisfaction in walking out the destiny and purpose He still has for you. Death and life…the two can truly merge together as we get past our own death caused by the loss of our child. In God's kingdom, life always comes from death. Allow God to plant His seed of hope right in the middle of your pain, and watch it grow into life.

Facing your pain is hard to do—it's never easy to face those things that make us feel so alone and broken. But every time we do, we grow a bit stronger, and we take one more step in the direction of healing.

No matter how broken you are today, tomorrow promises new hope.

Becca loved to sing and worship the Lord. She is four years old here, getting her hair back from the chemo, and using her little walker with one leg.

Becca leading worship. One of the hardest things for her to deal with was not having the use of her left hand to play the piano after her stroke.

CHAPTER 14

|||||||||||||||||||

Adding the Swimming Pool of Joy

I may be broken into what feels like a million pieces, but I don't want to be destroyed by this. Is that even possible? Does it make any sense?

I don't want to just survive; I want to learn how to thrive again. (And I wrote this line well before I ever heard a Christian song with a similar phrase.)

God's meaning of joy is not some euphoric happiness. It is an underlying belief that God is in control, and I can rejoice in His goodness and faithfulness at work in my life. Happiness is based on outward circumstances and can go away if those circumstances change; joy is based on a constant inner knowing of Truth, beyond the outward circumstances.

I think perhaps happiness is a feeling in our soul, and joy is a knowing in our spirit. The scriptural basis for this can be found in Galatians 5:22, which tells us one of the fruits of the Spirit in our lives is joy. In other words, the Holy Spirit produces joy in us. And where would that be? In our spirits, since we connect with God spirit-to-spirit. Happiness = soul fruit; Joy = spiritual fruit.

Seeds of Hope

I don't think it's possible to have joy without first having a seed of hope. Once you have hope, it is completely possible to go from there to a place of joy. Not only is it possible, but it is God's desire for us. He made a bridge between the two, and His name is Jesus Christ. Jesus Himself gave us His promise that with God, all things are possible (Matthew 19:26).

Let's tie Romans 8:25 and Hebrews 11:1 together. "If we hope for what we do not see, we eagerly wait for it with perseverance....Now faith is the substance of things hoped for, the evidence of things not seen."

In other words, hope is the seed that was planted to bring fruit or substance. We know it is there. We planted it ourselves with the guidance of the Holy Spirit. We have an assurance, a trust, a belief that cannot be shaken (faith). The seed of hope we cannot see is going to grow into a harvest we can see.

Hope is the seed planted, and joy is a fruit of that seed of hope.

I am not about to tell you that losing your child will turn into something joyous in your life. But I will tell you it is possible to have joy again in your life, beyond the grief. God says our grief can turn to joy. "You will be sorrowful, but your sorrow will be turned into joy" (John 16:20) is just one of many scriptures with a promise of mourning and sorrow being turned into joy in our lives. I choose to believe His Word, no matter what my feelings tell me at the moment. I choose to plant a seed of hope and watch it grow, being watered by His promises, and become the fruit of joy manifested in my life.

It is no secret the enemy works overtime to keep us from walking in joy. Why would he be so determined to steal my joy? Because God's joy is my strength. And I don't mean my joy in Him, I mean His joy in me. Most of us are familiar with Nehemiah 8:10, "…the joy of the Lord is your strength." In the English language (hang in here with me, now) the word "of" is a preposition. If I were to say, "This view *of the ocean* is our favorite," I would be referring to the ocean's view, right? If I were to say, "The book *of Kevin's* is lost," I would be referring to Kevin's book, right? Well, if the joy *of the Lord* is my strength, I see it referring to the Lord's joy, not mine!

When the Holy Spirit first showed me this, it was a *huge* relief! I don't have to manufacture or make sure I have joy (based on my love or my happiness in God) to have strength. My strength comes from knowing He is crazy in love with me! Wow! (Remember Zephaniah 3:17, how He is rejoicing over us with gladness and singing?) His joy over me is what makes me strong. His joy about me creates joy in me. Now there is a seed of hope to plant in your life for sure!

Another thing to help me get my joy back is something I alluded to in the beginning of the book: extending beyond my own grief and pain to help others. One of those people is someone I have yet to meet face-to-face, but we have a special love for each other. Her name is Hannah Linton, and she is the one who reached out to me through Facebook when her daughter Mercy was born prematurely. We continue to be in communication, encouraging each other and rejoicing and hurting together. No child can ever replace the pain and loss of another child, but

Hannah was very blessed to be able to have a baby after losing her precious little girl. This is a message I sent to her.

> I love seeing your beautiful family and how God has brought you to a wonderful place of joy. I know the pain is always ready to surface in a literal heartbeat, but life can go on and be full of, well, life!

Giving encouragement to Hannah has brought a measure of joy back into my life. Every time I can strengthen, offer hope, or help someone else in some way, it opens the door for more joy to be released. It is God's law of sowing and reaping. Giving is a spiritual act that bears spiritual fruit.

I have had to fight pretty hard when it comes to my joy. The enemy constantly tries to take it from me. Here is another key the Holy Spirit gave me, to help me fight and win this battle. While in Nigeria in May 2013, I wrote the following:

> Holy Spirit, why do I feel so out of sorts this morning? I feel agitated or irritated with the circumstances I find myself in. Lord, take these irritations and turn them into pearls. Help me to let go of them and just focus on You!

> *Laura, part of it is the enemy trying to blanket you with sadness about Becca and Kim. How can your mind and thoughts counter that? What are the good, godly things about them that bring joy to you? And what about the blessing of your sons? And your husband! Joy, My daughter! I speak great joy and great peace to you, My daughter!*

The Holy Spirit was reminding me that one of the keys to keeping my joy is being thankful. Whatever we focus on will consume us. If my thoughts and focus remain on my losses, the torment and pain will consume me. If my thoughts and focus are on the blessings I have, thankfulness and joy will consume me. So this key really goes back to what we already spent an entire chapter on: our thoughts.

The last key I want to share with you about being immersed in joy is the power of the Word of God. Several years ago I started praying for joy to have a stronger presence in my life. I looked up and wrote out eight pages of scriptures about joy and read through some of them every day for quite some time. I won't share all eight pages with you, but I definitely want to share a handful of these verses. (All of them are taken from the NIV.)

1 Chronicles 16:27 Splendor and majesty are before him; strength and joy are in his dwelling place.

Job 33:26 Then that person can pray to God and find favor with him, they will see God's face and shout for joy; he will restore them to full well-being.

Psalm 16:11 You make known to me the path of life; you will fill me with joy in your presence, with eternal pleasures at your right hand.

Psalm 30:11 You turned my wailing into dancing; you removed my sackcloth and clothed me with joy.

Psalm 51:12 Restore to me the joy of your salvation and grant me a willing spirit, to sustain me.

Psalm 86:4 Bring joy to your servant, Lord, for I put my trust in you.

Psalm 94:18-19 When I said, "My foot is slipping," your unfailing love, Lord, supported me. When anxiety was great within me, your consolation brought me joy.

Psalm 118:14-15 The Lord is my strength and my defense; he has become my salvation. Shouts of joy and victory resound in the tents of the righteous.

Isaiah 51:11 Those the Lord has rescued will return. They will enter Zion with singing; everlasting joy will crown their heads. Gladness and joy will overtake them, and sorrow and sighing will flee away.

Isaiah 61:3 ...to bestow on them a crown of beauty instead of ashes, the oil of joy instead of mourning, and a garment of praise instead of a spirit of despair. They will be called oaks of righteousness, a planting of the Lord for the display of his splendor.

John 15:10-11 If you keep my commands, you will remain in my love, just as I have kept my Father's commands and remain in his love. I have told you this so that my joy may be in you and that your joy may be complete.

Acts 2:28 You have made known to me the paths of life; you will fill me with joy in your presence.

Romans 12:11-12 ...keep your spiritual fervor, serving the Lord. Be joyful in hope, patient in affliction, faithful in prayer.

Romans 14:17 For the kingdom of God is not a matter of eating and drinking, but of righteousness, peace and joy in the Holy Spirit.

Romans 15:13 May the God of hope fill you with all joy and peace as you trust in him, so that you may overflow with hope by the power of the Holy Spirit.

Take time to meditate on these. Read them silently, read them out loud. Take a few words at a time and think about what those words mean for your life and how you can apply them.

I started this chapter with something I questioned regarding whether or not it made sense, and I will end it the same way. My joy is different now than it used to be. How is that possible? There isn't more than one kind of joy, is there? No, there isn't. I believe what has happened to me is that my joy is more of a solid undercurrent in my life now. It is built into the foundation and very fiber of my being. It has become a rock on which I am anchored. And the focus of where my joy comes from has shifted. It is now based on His joy over me, not my joy about Him.

Three Powerful Words

As I started writing this chapter, I knew three words I wanted to use to describe how I now sense joy in my life, but I was hesitant to say what those words are. I did not want to give anyone a false definition based on my experience. But as I was looking up the biblical definition of joy on the Internet, I found those exact three words.

So I now pass those three words on to you: contentment, confidence, and hope. May they become your words as well as you bravely dive into the swimming pool of joy.

CHAPTER 15

||||||||||||||

The Support Beam: A Word from Dave

The First Fog

It was dark, cold, and rainy that night as my two oldest sons, daughter-in-law, and I drove up to the University of Wisconsin Madison hospital. My wife and daughter Kim were already on their way up to visit Becca when they relayed the message that Becca had coded and the staff was trying to revive her. My thoughts scattered like the raindrops hitting the windshield. I had taken this same trip so many times over the past twenty-nine years, and had even heard those words before, but somehow I knew this time was different.

When I got off the fifth-floor elevator and turned the corner, I saw what would become a memory forever etched in my mind. Kim was standing in the hallway outside of Becca's room with that look I'll never forget. I asked, "Did she make it?" and she just shook her head no and fell into my arms. Kim was twenty-four at the time, but all I saw was my baby girl, hurting that her big sister was gone. I just held her and cried.

While I had my own feelings of finality about losing my first child, my initial thoughts were concern for my family, and I found myself asking God to surround them with His love and comfort. My eldest son, who grew up often arguing with his big sister, now lost his closest friend and companion. My baby girl in my arms was Becca's maid of honor and dreamed of the day Becca would be hers. My middle son was thankful that Becca had made his wedding two months earlier, but now she would never meet her nieces. And my youngest son, who was her ring bearer and now sixteen, would never get to have that adult relationship with her.

How was my wife doing? What about Becca's husband? And how would my granddaughter do, losing her mom at nine years old? All this was swirling through my head as I hugged my kids in the hallway. Of course there was my own pain, but my concern was for my family.

The next several days were a fog as we prepared for a funeral and tried to somehow come to grips with what just happened. It was like living in a foggy black-and-white movie with the exception of some vivid moments that jump out in dull colors in my memory. Each day brought new pain as we looked through photos to prepare for the visitation.

I have written many checks before, but I never dreamed I would be writing a check to pay for my daughter's burial plot! I could barely see through my tears to sign it.

Yet through all the sorrow, there were moments of great joy as well as we gathered as a family and told funny stories. It was very much an exhausting, emotional roller coaster.

Even as I wrote what I would say the day of the funeral, I had an amazing thought. When Rebecca was four, up on the fourth floor of the hospital receiving another week of chemo, in a small waiting room just outside her room, she accepted Jesus as her Savior. Now, twenty-five years later, in the very same hospital, she met Him face-to-face!

After the funeral, we followed the hearse in the processional across town to the cemetery. There we saw another one of those moments that jumped out of the fog. Seeing our three sons, especially our youngest, carrying their big sister's coffin to the gravesite…there are no words to describe it other than *this is just wrong!*

Daddy's Little Girl

Rebecca, or Becca-boo as we called her, was six months old when her mother and I started dating. She was two when Laura and I got married, and six months later I adopted her. She taught me the heart of our Father God toward us. Romans 8:15 talks about His adoption of us. My love for her was that of my "own" children. She got such a kick when people would tell her that she looked just like me or "you sure can tell she's your daughter!"

The start of our family

She wasn't always the easiest to live with, and definitely had some rough teen years, but on her wedding day she picked "Wind beneath My Wings" for our father/daughter dance. As we held each other close, she looked at me with tears in her eyes and sang to me the chorus, "Did you ever know that you're my hero?" She knew how to make her daddy cry! That moment we had was one I will never forget and is my absolute favorite picture of her and me.

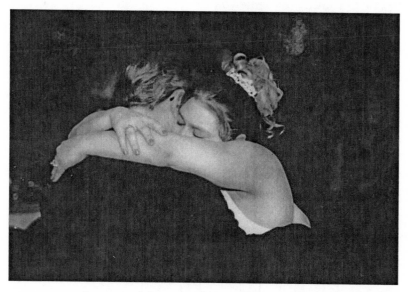

A very special moment between Dave and Becca

The last time she was in the hospital, I came home from work and felt an urgency to go visit her. I have to admit an embarrassing fact. I don't always recognize the voice of the Holy Spirit and sometimes just think it's me, but this time I listened and left to spend the evening with her. Unlike other times, it was just me and her. We talked and laughed, watched a little television—just had a great time together.

Before I left, I felt compelled to tell her something I never did before. I told her how she and I both knew she wasn't always easy to live with, but with all she had gone through—cancer, nine months of chemo, an above-knee amputation to deal with her whole life, her dangerous pregnancy, three open-heart surgeries, a stroke—I was always amazed at her zest for life, that smile on her face every day, and one of my favorite laughs. I reminded her of our father/daughter dance and how she sang to me, but it was important for her to know she was *my* hero! She told me with her sheepish big-eye grin, "I don't feel like it." I assured her that she was and how much I admired her.

When it was time to go, we gave each other a hug and kiss and said goodnight. On my way out, I looked at her and gave her the "I love you" sign with my hand, and as she did ever since she was little, she returned it and said, "I love you, Dad!" That was the last conversation we would ever have. I am so grateful I listened to that still small voice.

Allowing Myself to Grieve

Well, a couple of days after her funeral, it was time to go back to work. It was surreal as I was back in my normal surroundings and the world continued as it always had. Sure, a few people stopped in and gave me their condolences, but for the most part it was like nothing ever happened. I was still coming in and out of this fog. *How do I go back to the day-to-day and act like nothing has changed?*

I believe most of us men tend to compartmentalize everything in our minds. Mark Gungor (*Laugh Your Way to a Better Marriage*) says we have tiny little boxes that we take out ever so gently so as to not disturb any other boxes. I think this is a pretty accurate description of me. For the most part, I was able to take out my work box and stay there, but grief had just shattered my "Becca box" into a million pieces. I tried to sweep my grief into a grief box, but the problem with grief is that it cannot stay in a box! Somehow those shattered pieces find a way into all the other boxes. These pieces tend to appear out of nowhere and not always at convenient times.

It was not easy, and at times I would close my door and allow myself to tear up and grieve some more. So if you're reading this and you're a father who has lost a child and you tend to compartmentalize, I encourage you to allow yourself those moments to grieve. Grieving is not a sign of weakness, it is a way for us to heal.

The following Sunday morning, I was playing my saxophone for worship service as usual. We sang "No Sweeter Name than the Name of Jesus" by Kari Jobe. It was a song I usually sang as a duet with Becca during worship. I tried to sing it this time, but it was hard. When it came to my sax solo, I just allowed the tears to flow as I played from my heart. I wanted my worship to join in with the angels and saints in heaven (including my daughter). It may have been one of the most anointed times ever, because I allowed myself to be vulnerable, which opened others' hearts to worship our Lord.

Becca's heart of worship, and worshiping with her, is one of the things I miss the most. After service, it was a beautiful day so I took my tenor and soprano saxophones to the gravesite and played several songs we would minister together with, including two of the songs she wrote that I loved the most, "Do You Feel the Wind of the Spirit?" and the one inscribed on her tombstone, "Before the Throne." I played my heart out with no one else in sight, switching from horn to horn and hearing them echo through the woods. To this day, when I play I think of the reality that my praise is joining hers and so many others around His throne! It is an awesome thought.

Another specific day at the gravesite that is etched in my memory is the first Father's Day after her death. All holidays brought some difficulty as we celebrated Christmas, New Year's, and family birthdays including hers, but Father's Day was different for me. Becca was the child who made me a father when she was two and I adopted her. I vividly remember her bringing me donuts for breakfast in bed for my first Father's Day. Now, this day was my first one without her. I had four other children whom I loved dearly and spent the day with, but I needed to spend time at her graveside that day as well. It was probably the longest time I ever stayed out there. Just reminiscing, crying tears of pain that she wasn't with us anymore, tears of joy for all the funny memories. I needed to allow myself that time of grief.

One thing I personally struggled with while at the grave was talking to Becca. Many people, including my wife, find it natural and helpful to talk to their child as if they are there. I have no problem with others doing that as even Hebrews 12:1 tells us "we are surrounded by such a great cloud of witnesses," as though those who have gone before us are cheering us on. But I have always found it hard to believe that while in His glorious presence in heaven, my loved ones would (if they could) have time or even think to look or listen to what I'm doing on earth. I believe this is just one of those things we will never really know until we get there. However, it was frustrating because I, like anyone, would have loved to be able to let her know how much I loved her and that she would not be forgotten.

A few weeks after Becca's death, I took my sons to see the movie *Courageous*. I told them that I knew it was about a dad who changed his priorities in life after his little girl died. While we watched it, we hit the scene where they are in the hospital hallway and learn that she died. All four of us were overcome with tears as it was so much like that night in the hospital. Even the coffin in the movie looked similar to Becca's. My oldest left the theater and did not return; the other two came back in after a while. I told them I was sorry that this was so painful to watch and so close to what we experienced, but I felt compelled to watch it. I felt God had something to show me through this, no matter how painful.

And then later in the film, there it was. The dad stopped by the park where earlier his daughter wanted him to dance with her. He refused because he felt so stupid, so she danced by herself as he watched. Now, after her death, he played the song she danced to without him, but this time he danced in the park as if she were in his arms. Afterwards, he tearfully asked God to tell his little girl that he finally danced with her! That may seem simple to you, but to me it was profound. Maybe Becca isn't able to see and hear me for whatever reasons in my head, but one thing I have no doubt of: if I ask Jesus to relay a message from me to her, He will! He cares that much for us!

Bathed in Grace

I cannot overemphasize how important it was for me to make allowances for my family members, especially my wife, in the way they processed their grief. We all handle grief in different ways and on different timelines. My other four children all grieved in different ways and some longer than others. They all still have times when they miss Becca immensely. I encourage all of them to allow each other the space they need to grieve in their own way and not expect the others to grieve in the same way they themselves do.

This is especially true for us husbands in regard to our wives. If you are like me, as I suspect many men are, I didn't always want to talk about it. I preferred to keep my feelings to myself, except with a few close people. My wife, on the other hand, seemed to wear her grief on her sleeve. Actually that's an interesting saying because once in our society we literally did wear our grief on our sleeve by wearing black armbands. Maybe it's something we should think about bringing back, but I digress.

My wife would post all sorts of feelings on Facebook. I would every so often, but nothing like she did or does. So much so that I knew it made some people uncomfortable, even though she always pointed to God as her source of strength. I would sometimes think *is this normal* or *is my wife having some major issues here?*

Laura has the closest relationship to God of anyone I know. She amazes me with her insight, yet here she was struggling even though she knew without a doubt where Becca was and the glory she was experiencing. Was it normal for this to be so hard and go on so long? Truth is, absolutely! Pretty much everything is "normal" when it comes to grief, it seems.

I think often as men we want to get past difficult things quickly and then "get on with life," at least to one degree or another. But I believe that, as devastating as the loss of a child is to a father, it is even more intense for a mother. There is no other relationship on earth like that of a mother and her child. We all know and understand how she carries that child for up to nine months in her womb.

But what we often miss is that not only is she carrying the body of another human being, but she is carrying inside her the very soul and spirit of that human being! Once that baby is born, the umbilical cord is cut and the child's body is separated from mommy, but I believe that soul tie and spiritual connection is never cut.

I believe this is one of the main reasons it can be so painful for a mother who loses her baby during pregnancy. People may wonder how she can be so emotionally attached to a child she never met or held. But there was that soul and spirit connection that we may never fully understand this side of heaven. I think most women in that situation will tell you it is very real.

In many cases, if not most, it will take our wives months or years to "get on with life" the way we imagine they should. But it isn't our place to determine what that looks like; ours is to simply love, care for, and protect her during this time, however long it may be. It even occurred to me that often people, myself included, criticize those who post too many feelings on Facebook. I wonder, though, what we would think of King David's posts if he were one of our "friends." The Psalms look quite a bit like some Facebook postings, and they are plastered with his feelings!

My Final Thoughts

Losing a child is like an amputation. A part of your very being has been cut off from you. You will never be the same, but you will learn to function again.

When Becca had her amputation as a toddler, it was one of the most traumatic things her little body could go through. There were times when she would feel phantom pains (when the leg that was gone would feel like it was hurting or itching). It took a while for the body and brain to get used to missing that leg. It took time and strength and the will to carry on, but Becca learned to live her life, forever changed, but an amazing life anyway. She had a calling on her life, and losing that leg was not going to stop her.

It can be that way spiritually for parents, especially moms, after losing a child. It can be the most horrific thing to go through. It takes time to heal. It takes time to learn how to function without our child. But even though a part of you has died with them, you can live your life again. The effects of that loss will always be there, but God loves you more than you could ever fathom and still has a purpose for you. Just like little Becca, in time you can go on with an amazing life that can touch others. Forever changed by the loss, but also forever changed by the inheritance your child left you.

In our case, she left us a beautiful granddaughter. Another granddaughter was named after her. The memories of her laughter and her worship songs fill my heart. Take time to think of all the many things you inherited from your child. Embrace them!

The greatest joy I have is looking at the plaque we have on the wall, where Laura and myself and all our children promised each other when one of us goes on to heaven before the others, we will *B-There*! That we accept the gift of salvation Jesus gave us and live our lives to the fullest to serve Him until that day so that we too will *B-There* with Him and those in our family who went before us. I look at that almost every day and am so glad she made that promise to us and us to her. No better inheritance than to be there together!

CHAPTER 16

|||||||||||||||||

Out in the Driveway... Where Do I Go from Here?

Working through our grief is *a lot* of hard work.

To get to the other side of this, we have to move through it, with no exceptions. There is no map and no expert guide telling us whether to turn left, right, north, or south. But there are others, like myself, who are just a few steps ahead of you on the same path. We have had to navigate through this on our own individual map of life, but we can at least direct you to some road signs along your way.

Road Sign #1: Let Go

One road sign we all have to follow at some point (if we want to quit wandering in our painful hopelessness) is to let go. I am not talking about letting go of your child but letting go to release yourself. They are not the same thing. To let go in this way doesn't mean you don't care. It doesn't mean putting your child behind you and forgetting. That will never happen. Letting go and releasing yourself means you are no longer willing to allow your grief to control your life, especially to the point of not being able to function.

Road Sign #2: Release Your Guilt to Go Forward

We also have to get past the road sign of feeling guilty for going on with our lives, allowing ourselves to be happy and laugh again. It is not, I repeat NOT, betraying our son or daughter to purposefully go forward with our lives!

The following question did not help me personally, but I have heard of many parents it has helped, so I will ask: Would your child want to know that his or her death caused your life to come to a permanent standstill? How guilty would they feel knowing they ruined your life? Would your child want you to stay in this dark, depressing place? Or would he or she say, "Just because I am not there on earth with you anymore does not mean you can't get past this darkness and live the full and wonderful life God wants to bless you with." Wouldn't you rather show how deeply you love your child by pressing through, little by little, until you can have a full life with joy and laughter once again?

Is it possible you are actually dishonoring your child by staying stuck in this place of deep grief and pain? The best way to honor your child is to *live*!

Many of you were not able to say goodbye to your child as I was (even though I did not know it was a final earthly goodbye). I cannot even begin to imagine what it would be like if things were left unsaid, or it happened at a time when the relationship was strained for whatever reason. My heart goes out to those of you with that kind of added pain.

Can I make a suggestion? Write your child a letter. Write about how much you hurt. Write about how much you miss him. Write about how sorry you are you didn't get to say goodbye to her, or about what it was that put friction between the two of you. Write as many details as you want to write. Make it as many pages as you want it to be. Cry as many tears as you want to cry as you write it. Forgive your precious child for his or her part in it, and accept forgiveness from them for yourself.

Then destroy the letter. This is not something you want to revisit and read over and over again. It is something you are using as a tool to release yourself. So get rid of it, as a symbol of letting yourself go.

Road Sign #3: No Timeline

Here's another road sign many of us need for guidance. Sometimes we seem to put ourselves on a timeline of grief, with a date or length of time by which we think we should be done grieving. And I have never heard of anyone who has gotten this predetermined timeline right. Every parent, including myself, has said it takes a lot longer than they ever thought it would. It's more than okay to miss the deadline you set up for yourself.

From everything I have heard and read, I have actually gone through a fairly quick process. One reason is because of what I discovered when I started reading books to find out what it was like for other bereaved parents. So many of those books were about parents who were still in a place of darkness and depression (the suffocating black hole that sucks you under) many years later. Some of those books made me feel hopeless, like I would never have a life again. And as you know, I simply refused to believe that! I refused to believe my life ended when Becca's life ended. I knew that I knew that I knew I was still here for a reason. My life still had a purpose, and I had to find a way to get past this blackness, to be able to live the life God had put me here on earth to live.

So I purposely worked through my pain, and worked through the mourning, and worked through the worst of the grieving. Unfortunately, I don't think any of us will ever be fully on the other side of our grief while here on earth. From everything I can tell, it is a process we will go through for the rest of our earthly lives. But I refuse to let it debilitate me, causing me to miss out on my family and on fulfilling my God-given destiny.

You Must Make a Choice

Please hear my heart, as I say this once again as gently as I can, but there comes a point when we must make a choice. We either choose to stay in our black hole (letting it become our identity for our remaining time here on earth), or we refuse to stay in this place (grabbing hold of hope as a lifeline, allowing God to help us out of this evil dark pit we have been thrown into).

You can be sure He does not want us to stay there. But the decision is left up to us when, or if, we want to come out. As soon as we decide we want out, He will be right there as our Helper and Guide. There are times we will be given a rope to pull us, and other times we will have to do our own climbing, but it is worth it! It is worth choosing to come out of the black pit up to a lighted path, to be a part of the lives of our other children, of our spouse, of our grandchildren, of other family members, of our friends, and of those we have yet to meet. LIFE IS WORTH LIVING AGAIN!

What about prayer? Why haven't I talked much about prayer? I have, throughout the entire book. Most of the journal entries you read were written prayers. I hope you know by now we can tell God anything, including how angry we are at Him.

Many years ago my youngest daughter was really struggling with some things. She swore at God, telling Him she wasn't sure she even believed in Him. When my daughter shared this with me, I couldn't help but smile on the inside. You see, it proved deep down she knew she could trust Him with her deepest darkest thoughts. He already knows what we are thinking and how we are feeling. You might as well have it out with Him. He can take it. And once it is out in the open between you, He can tell you what He is thinking and how He is feeling. I guarantee it will be exactly what you need to hear, full of grace, mercy, and love.

Thankfully, prayer is more than just time set aside every morning before starting your day, or a set gathering at church. Prayer is an ongoing conversation with God that can take place at any time, in any place. Talk to Him from your heart throughout the day, and then listen for His response. He is there, and He wants to be in communication with you. As you become more and more aware of His presence, you will occasionally hear Him initiate the conversation. You will be amazed at the healing that happens in those beautiful random moments of prayer.

An Unexpected Road Sign

Be sure to look for the road signs of hope God is holding out for you. I know you already read an entire chapter on this subject, but it is worth bringing up again. Here is a sign of hope I found God giving me at one point. A lifelong friend gave me a devotional book, and for some reason one of the things I wanted to do right away was read what was written for October 12, the day Becca left us. That entry did not touch me nearly as much as the one for October 11 did, directly across the page.

First, it reminded me how God is the Alpha and Omega. (For many years I have declared through prayer that He is the Alpha and Omega. He is the beginning and the end, which means He has the final word on *everything*.)

Then it continued as if God Himself were speaking to me about my precious Becca, the day before she went to be with Him forever. I read how He was shielding Becca with His presence, holding her in His loving arms. He was taking her from the world's darkness into His light. And she was to rest in knowing she is now complete in Him and will always be in His presence.

I circled it and wrote the words "Becca's last full day on earth" at the top of the page. I still can't get over the truth of this for her now, and the date it appeared in this little devotional book. Thank You, God, for these precious little rays of hope You send our way, to bring us out of our place of darkness.

Then there was the page in the same devotional book for October 13, the day after Becca died. God used it to tell me to take time to be still in His presence...to breathe...to receive the peace He was offering me...to hide that peace in my heart and let it grow in me and not let my circumstances take it from me.

Even now as I read that page and write these words, I feel God's peace growing inside me and His love wrapping around me, even though tears once again are finding their way down my face.

If you don't know God in this way, you can if you want to. He has been waiting for you, His heart breaking for you, wanting to comfort you, bring you stillness and peace that cannot be explained or understood, and to just love on you in a way you have never known or been able to even imagine. Open yourself up to Him by telling Him you want and need Him in your life. Let Him know you believe and accept the price Jesus paid for your sin, which was to die as a sacrifice in your place. Ask Him to forgive you of your sins and to come live inside of you. Tell Him you are putting Him in charge of your life and surrendering to His ways, believing that as your Creator He has a special plan for your life.

If you are not familiar with the Bible, or don't know where to access more information to help you grow in this new life with God inside you, please go to our ministry website (see the Resource section) where you will find things to read and resources to help you walk this new path you are on.

It will be important for you to find a place where other believers in Christ get together on a regular basis, people you can spend time with who will help you grow and get stronger. God already has a place picked out for you, so be sure to ask Him to lead you to that place.

I found this written in my journal a year after we lost Becca. As I look at it now I can see how much it applies to us who are grieving the loss of our children.

I saw in the vision a river, with heaven and glory in the distance. Everyone had to make a decision whether they were going to swim and fight their way to the kingdom, or float there. Everyone would get there eventually, but some wanted the easy way and just float. Sometimes there were whitewater rapids and the floaters would capsize. They could choose to get back on their flotation device or boat, or they could choose to start swimming. Those who swam and fought the waters got to the kingdom quicker than those who were floating, but it was a lot of work. We can float to the kingdom and get there eventually, or we can swim and fight the water and get there sooner.

Take a minute and think about this. We all have to "go the distance." We all have to get through to the end of our lives, no matter how short or long that will be. When our child died, it tossed us out into whitewater rapids, and we need to get through to the other side where the waters are much calmer. We can get back into a raft and float with a false security (hopefully getting to those calmer waters eventually), or we can swim and fight our way through, getting there sooner. Obviously the swimming is work, but if we decide to just float along, continuing to be tossed and dumped, how much will we miss out on because of how far back in the river we still are? Yes, there are times we need the raft. But there are also times we will get to the calm waters quicker by swimming. I hope you will decide there are times worth swimming and fighting your way through so you can live to the fullest potential possible after such deep brokenness and devastation.

If you are hoping I will tell you at some point there will be closure, I have to disappoint you. I have never heard of a parent getting closure. Maybe they eventually found out the details of their child's death, or a perpetrator received a guilty verdict in the courtroom, but it didn't bring closure. Not like other people talk about in the death of a parent or spouse or someone else. As a parent, we never close that part of our life. It becomes something that molds us into a different person than we were before. There is no closure, just a change in who we are, and now we are left to figure out who that is.

Bad things happen to good people. Horrible and evil things happen to God's people. You have paid what many will say is the ultimate price of sacrifice on this earth—the death of your son or daughter. (Sound familiar? I know someone else who paid the price of His Son a little over two thousand years ago.) But you did not give your child willingly, or have a choice.

The question is: Are you going to let it be a wasted sacrifice? Are you going to become bitter or better? What value are you going to place on the life of your child? That is where the mind shift happens. Life or death? Becca not only died, she had life! Maybe your child didn't have twenty-nine years of life, maybe he only had sixteen, or maybe she only had seven, or maybe your child did not even have life outside of your womb, but there was still LIFE! Because I had the blessing and honor of giving Becca life, I choose to LIVE to honor her life.

I refuse to let death cause more death! I will NOT give the enemy that kind of a victory! Because Jesus lives, I can live. I have allowed my God to make good on His promises in my life, to give strength to the weary and hope to the hopeless. And I will allow that hope to continue to grow as it becomes joy that reaches beyond death, both my child's and mine.

Becca Diehl class of 2000

POSTLUDE

||||||||||||

If you would like to continue along the subject of parental grief, you might be interested in taking a look at what else I have written.

From Ring Bearer to Pallbearer

Siblings grieve through a different lens, often completely unrecognized by the world. Some are even told to "look after their parents" as though they are fine with their loss and can be a strong support to others. This is so very wrong and painful.

Another virtually forgotten group in the loss of a child is the grandparents. They not only lost their grandchild but have to watch their own child go through the trauma and blackness, trying to survive the loss.

With this in mind, I have put together a small book titled *From Ring Bearer to Pallbearer*, with thoughts from our sons and our parents. It includes a beautiful poem our oldest son wrote for his sister after her death. I feel it is important for all of them to have a voice to share their hearts, offering their experience of losing a sister and losing a granddaughter.

This book can easily be given to those who have experienced the same loss of a sibling or a grandchild. It is a way to personally acknowledge the intense pain of their loss, which is way too often ignored, while pointing them to someone who can relate to their pain through personal experience. *From Ring Bearer to Pallbearer* can be found exclusively at *www.gpshope.org* as a free PDF download (just register for our free library membership).

Come Grieve Through Our Eyes

There is no magical age when the death of our child doesn't affect us in a very deep and profound way. Whether our child died in the womb or was in their sixties, the wrongness of their death causes trauma, and we are never the same.

Most of our grief is done behind closed doors, which is why I have also written the book *Come Grieve through Our Eyes: An Open Door into the Life of Grieving Parents*. The contents capture the raw emotions and actual words of dozens of bereaved parents, talking about subjects those who have not experienced the death of a child don't understand, or may not think about. The following is an excerpt from this book.

Why Won't They Let Me Talk About My Child?

As bereaved parents, we have a need to keep our child's memory alive. One of the ways we do that is to talk about our child. Other people eventually don't talk about them, and we don't hear their names come up in conversations any more. And if the child was young, not very many people had a chance to know our child, so the conversations about them are even fewer. Often, the lack of hearing people acknowledge our child's life intensifies our

*need to talk about them, which people around us often do
not understand.*

*Child loss is a trauma -- a heartbreaking trauma
-- and parents need to be able to talk freely about their
child. Quite often they are shut off by others who don't
want to listen by changing the subject abruptly, or simply
saying, "You're living too much in the past."*

*One of the best ways others can help is to simply be
good listeners. Allow parents to tell their story as often as they
feel the need, and that includes being okay with any tears.*

*Here is what grieving parents have to say about
this subject...*

In *Come Grieve Through Our Eyes*, I introduce the term
"pareavor", a word for parents who have lost a child through
death. It explains why the word is needed, and how I came up
with the term. (Note: The word pareavor was not used in *When
Tragedy Strikes*, as it was actually written before *Come Grieve Through
Our Eyes*.).

The feedback and endorsements have been very positive,
especially from those who have lost a child. They are thrilled
to have something to put in the hands of those around them,
giving them a voice. As a pareavor, I encourage you to get a
copy of *Come Grieve through Our Eyes: An Open Door into the Life of
Grieving Parents* for yourself, and a second one to pass along to
someone whom you want to have a better understanding of
the masks we wear and why we wear them. It can also be a tool
for pastors and those who want to know how to help grieving
parents beyond supplying meals for a couple of weeks and a
having a balloon launch.

Come Grieve through Our Eyes can be found on Amazon and Kindle, among other places.

A Final Word

My prayer is that after reading *When Tragedy Strikes* you can now see more light in the darkness, and have hope in your future. You *can* allow God to make good on His promises to give strength to the weary and hope to the hopeless. You *can* have life again, after the death of your child. It is a long process, often three steps forward and two-and-a-half steps back. But when that happens, you are still ahead by half a step.

I would be honored to continue this journey with you. If you want to connect with me on a more personal level, please add yourself to our GPS Hope Facebook page, and also take a look around on our GPS Hope website, where you will find other ways to connect with us (including occasional web chats and information about occasional get-away retreats).

We are always looking for ways to bring hope and encouragement to bereaved parents, and would love to hear from you if you have any suggestions or other good resources you have discovered.

I want to end this book by coming into agreement with God's Word over your life. *For I know the thoughts that I think toward you, says the Lord, thoughts of peace and not of evil, to give you a future and a hope* (Jeremiah 29:11).

ABOUT THE AUTHOR

||||||||||||||||||||||||||||||||||||||||||||||||

Laura Diehl, along with her husband, Dave, lives in Southern Wisconsin. They are the founders of GPS Hope: Grieving Parents Sharing Hope, which extends hope and healing to all grieving parents through a growing list of resources and a loving community to encourage one another in their unique, difficult journey.

Laura is also the author of *Triple Crown Transformation* (published in 2015), which is based on her many tragic life experiences, to help others learn the lessons she has been taught in three areas: See the Crown, Wear the Crown, Be the Crown. This book is the foundation of Crown of Glory Ministries, also founded by Dave and Laura, which encourages and equips the body of Christ to find their rightful royal place in God's kingdom.

"Kidz Korner" is a monthly article published for Impact Ministries International, written by Laura for children. It is based on her many years of children's ministry experience, encouraging kids to go deeper in their relationship with the Holy Spirit.

Laura loves to travel, which is good because she has traveled as an ordained minister for many years both nationally and internationally. She is available as an author, speaker, minister, and teacher and can be contacted by email at laura@ crownofgloryministries.org.

More information about GPS Hope or Crown of Glory Ministries can be found in the Resource section.

RESOURCES

|||||||||||||||||

www.gpshope.org

On the GPS Hope website you will be able to access the following:

- *From Ring Bearer to Pallbearer: Thoughts from Grieving Siblings and Grandparents* (book)
- Joy scriptures
- A list of recommended books for grieving parents
- Occasional video messages
- Dates and information for occasional video chats
- Dates and information for occasional GPS Hope events (get-away retreats, etc.)
- Other miscellaneous items

https://www.facebook.com/groups/GPSHope
www.crownofgloryministries.org
www.facebook.com/crownofgloryministries.laura
http://thecomfortcub.com

Jesus Calling: Enjoying Peace in His Presence by Sarah Young. Give yourself the gift of this book; you won't be sorry.

CPSIA information can be obtained
at www.ICGtesting.com
Printed in the USA
FFOW05n0505061215